Warwick University Caribbean Studies

V

Theo   ~proaches To
West Ina...n Fiction By Women

Evelyn O'Callaghan

MACMILLAN
CARIBBEAN

First published 1993

Published by THE MACMILLAN PRESS LTD
London and Basingstoke
Associated companies and representatives in Accra,
Auckland, Delhi, Dublin, Gaborone, Hamburg, Harare,
Hong Kong, Kuala Lumpur, Lagos, Manzini, Melbourne,
Mexico City, Nairobi, New York, Singapore, Tokyo.

ISBN 0–333–57837–6

Printed in Hong Kong

A catalogue record for this book is available from the
British Library.

Cover based on a painting by Aubrey Williams presented to
The Centre for Caribbean Studies, University of Warwick.

Series preface

This is the first book in this series to focus specifically on West Indian women. By studying their writings we are taken to the heart of rarely analysed aspects of Caribbean society. Although concentrating on anglophone writers, many of the issues discussed here reflect womens' experiences throughout the whole region. If we wish to understand the problems which afflict the Caribbean we cannot afford to neglect the insights which women writers have to offer, as they can often illuminate social and economic experiences more graphically than many an arid social science analysis.

Although there have been forerunners to the contemporary explosion of West Indian womens' writing, these have remained largely invisible and inadequately represented in anthologies as West Indian literature has tended in the past to be male-dominated. This book challenges stereotypes by discussing, from a woman's viewpoint, issues such as the colonial legacies of racism, class and patriarchalism, as well as educational influence, generational tensions, problems of the 'white outsider' and of sexuality. Formal innovations are also analysed: the breaching of genre boundaries, experiments to escape from writing in the 'master's' tongue by mining the rich seams of oral traditions and Creole speech and by using fluidities of style as an alternative to the tyranny of linear realistic narrative.

Repudiating the notion that womens' writing is a 'literature of opposition' Evelyn O'Callaghan argues for an aesthetic of pluralism and a 'creolised' critical theory.

Alistair Hennessy
Series Editor

Warwick University Caribbean Studies

Series Editor: Alistair Hennessy

For Stewart Brown, and
for Philip

Contents

Acknowledgements

I would like to acknowledge the support of my colleagues in the Department of English, University of the West Indies, Cave Hill Campus, who took on extra work so that I could have 'time off' to start this book; the help of the Women and Development Studies Group of the University of the West Indies, in granting me funds towards typing the manuscript; Sandra Taylor, for *doing* the typing and revisions under pressure; Glyne Griffith, Denise deCaries Narain and especially Jane Bryce, for reading and offering invaluable advice on several chapters; and my family, who gave me space, time and encouragement.

Note

All bracketed numbers are the *page* numbers of the particular text referred to in the current sentence or sentences.

The author and publishers wish to thank the following who have kindly given permission for the use of copyright material:
Longman Group UK Limited for an extract from 'Lily, Lily' from *Arrival of the Snake Woman and Other Stories* by Olive Senior.
New Beacon Books Limited for extracts from *Poems of Succession* by Martin Carter.
Virago Press for extracts from *Whole of a Morning Sky* by Grace Nichols.
The Women's Press Limited for an extract from *Considering Women* by Velma Pollard.

Introduction

Women poets

the little man
too early home today
surprised me scribbling
while the washer turned
ahaa . . . I see you
take your little write
well let me see your book . . .
mhmm . . . mhmm . . . not bad not bad
a little comma here
a period there
that sentence can make sense . . .
almost

your friend there scribbling too
and Genie down the road
well well how nice
how triply nice
not mad not mad . . .

Velma Pollard (1989: xi)

The obligatory 'personal statement'

When I first began to study West Indian fiction in the 1970s, I was under the impression that there were no women writers from the region apart from Jean Rhys, *and* there was some reservation about her. But when I joined the English Department at the Mona Campus of the University of the West Indies, in the early 1980s, Mervyn Morris introduced me to Erna Brodber's *Jane and Louisa Will Soon Come Home*, recently published. My learning experience had begun. Since then I have been lucky enough to live at a time when anglophone Caribbean (West Indian)[1] women's writing finally achieved 'publisher credibility' and there was no shortage of material by talented women to keep me reading.

Yet the texts chosen for teaching at the University tended to remain those of the 'big boys' (Brathwaite and Walcott and Carter, Lamming and Naipaul and Harris) with Rhys's *Wide Sargasso Sea* the only female-authored text. By the end of the 1980s, more and more West Indian women writers had gained local and international recognition, and a few of their works filtered into the syllabus. By 1991, now at the Cave Hill Campus of the University, I decided the time had come to devote at least one course entirely to this writing, and met with no objections, despite the fact that this was the first such offering. Most of my students were West Indian women, and I thought they would welcome the chance to sample a selection of prose works – from *Wide Sargasso Sea* (1966) to Olive Senior's *Arrival of the Snake Woman and Other Stories* (1989) – as a group. It is out of this teaching experience that the ideas in this book began to clarify.

Comparative literature courses which include women writers from the francophone and hispanophone territories are still on the drawing board, though a sprinkling of their books are taught in the Departments of French and Spanish. Of the available anthologies of West Indian and Caribbean prose,[2] only Mordecai and Wilson's *Her True True Name* (1989) and Esteves and Paravisini-Gebert's *Green Cane and Juicy Flotsam* (1991) are devoted entirely to women writers, and their cross-Caribbean focus is far more rewarding than my specifically West Indian one. However, time constraints and my linguistic (in)competence limited me to the more familiar territory, and my students' preference for prose led to the choice of fiction rather than poetry for the course.

In terms of critical material, women's writing receives minimal attention in classic works like Ramchand's *The West Indian Novel and its Background* (1970) and Michael Gilkes's *The West Indian Novel* (1981); Jean Rhys warrants a chapter in Bruce King's *West Indian Literature* (1979) and of the eighteen pieces in Edward Baugh's *Critics on Caribbean Literature* (1978), only one deals with a female writer: the poet Louise Bennett. So we were very fortunate that two pioneering works on regional women's fiction had just been published: Carole Davies and Elaine Fido's *Out of the Kumbla* (1990) and Selwyn Cudjoe's *Caribbean Women Writers* (1990). Susheila Nasta's *Motherlands* (1991 and 1992), which is a more comparative collection of critical essays on women writers from Africa, the Caribbean and South Asia soon followed. In addition, I used articles and essays on the writers from various sources, and I hope this book will save others some of the initial footwork!

The critical approach to West Indian women's fiction is, generally speaking, feminist, mine included, and that was the line I took in suggesting textual readings to the students; the difficulty of defining what 'brand' of feminism was yet another motivation for this extended study. I have to say that while my, mostly female, students were vocal in identifying with the material and emotional experiences of the fictional protagonists, they were a bit more wary of the political conclusions I read into these experiences. None the less, there was no shortage of debate and discussion and, in time, I trust they too will privilege female-authored works in their own teaching practice so that none of *their* students will think, as I did, that West Indian women don't write good/publishable books.

Initial conclusions

I offer a synopsis of our tentative findings at the end of the course, as to recurring thematic and stylistic features in the fictions, as a useful starting point for this book, and for others who come to the reading and analysis of the literature. Most of the features mentioned below will be developed in later chapters.

Most importantly, West Indian women's fiction foregrounds women: a truism, perhaps, but notable given the male-dominated nature of Caribbean literature in general, with female representation usually consisting of consolidation of stereotype or relegation to the periphery of narrative. Women writers frequently – especially in their first books – utilize the perspective of a girl-child/adolescent, and my students enthusiastically, and sometimes bitterly, endorsed the authenticity of the texts' treatment of problematic adult/child relations. The whole issue of 'mothering' (not necessarily by biological mother) is central in this literature, and is often treated ambivalently: the novels of Jamaica Kincaid, Merle Hodge and Paule Marshall's *Brown Girl, Brownstones*, are cases in point. Nasta's *Motherlands* is particularly helpful, not to say ingenious, in teasing out some of the ramifications of mother/mothering/motherland in the texts.

Given the Caribbean's history of colonization, and the ubiquitous 'quest for identity' theme in its literature, it is hardly surprising that the women's writing, too, is concerned with the influences of race and class hierarchies, the legacy of slavery and colonial hegemony. However, the women writers *also* note how race and class inform socialization into gender, and what problems result. In the work of Merle Collins, Janice Shinebourne and Zee Edgell, for example, the combination of racist, 'classist' and patriarchal prejudices is demonstrably detrimental to a female sense of self, and divides instead of uniting women (Tia and Antoinette in *Wide Sargasso Sea*). In some cases, psychological damage is so severe as to drive female protagonists to insanity and self-destruction, a subject I explore in Chapter 2.

A related topic is the journey to and/or relationship with the 'Mother Country', and the exploration of the love/hate relationship which several protagonists experience with the metropole, the imperial centre. Of course, novels of migration and 'exile' have been written by West Indians since they started to trek to 'foreign' in search of a better life, and since many contemporary women writers live for extended periods abroad (Joan Riley, Jamaica Kincaid, Michelle Cliff), the opposing pulls between 'motherland' and 'Mother Country' will no doubt continue to receive fictional articulation. While authorial affirmation tends to be squarely behind Caribbean (mother) culture, the foreign-based women writers bring to their work new perspectives on 'home' as well as searching questions about their place in the metropole: Joan Riley's *The Unbelonging* and Elean Thomas's *The Last Room* are good examples. In this, as in other aspects, West Indian women's fiction demonstrates concrete points of reference with that of African and Afro-American woman, with Paule Marshall's *Praise Song for the Widow* linking all three.

Since colonial culture was chiefly transmitted via the middle-class values and aspirations enshrined in an inherited educational system, the alienating effects of schooling, usually buttressed by the teachings of an authoritarian Christianity, have long been targeted in Caribbean literature. Again, by foregrounding female experience, women writers reveal the ways in which restrictive gender roles imbue colonial ideology, and are enforced through the educational process. Olive Senior's stories, as well as Merle Hodge's *Crick Crack Monkey* and Jamaica Kincaid's *Annie John* dramatize this insidious conditioning. Furthermore, in these and other texts, older women *within* the community are indicted for supporting and transmitting the damaging ethics (conform, submit) that are the implicit goals of a 'good Christian education' for girls; this feature receives further treatment in Chapter 3. However, it should be noted that the grandmother figure (as in *Annie John* and *Crick Crack Monkey*) is frequently an exception, serving as a model of strength, self-confidence and fighting spirit for the young female protagonist.

Crucial to this type of schooling for 'young ladies', with its Victorian strictures as to respectability and morality, is an underlying taboo on the expression of female sexuality. Several writers depict the resulting problematizing of sexuality for young women coming to an awareness of their maturing bodies. Sexuality is for them associated with shame, defilement and the forced renunciation of childhood freedom (with its relative androgyny) for what is perceived to be the dangerous vulnerability of female adulthood. In *Jane and Louisa* and *Annie John*, the realization that maturity involves becoming a gendered sexual being is a traumatic one; in Zee Edgell's *Beka Lamb*, the consequences of a woman's 'fall' into sexuality are tragically brought home to the young protagonist.

Implicitly or overtly, West Indian women's fiction re-examines and counters several female stereotypes, and the second part of *Out of the Kumbla* is a helpful guide to the various literary strategies utilized in this project. Obviously, one method of refusing or subverting patriarchal myths and stereotypes is the creation of complex and multi-faceted female subjects. Jeremy Poynting (1990) discusses tensions between gender and ethnic identity in portrayals of Indo-Caribbean women, and in Chapter 1 I focus on how writings by selected white women call into question stereotypical placings of the 'white' creole woman simply as peripheral 'mistress' of the plantation house.

The general presentation of male-female relationships in the writing, as Mordecai and Wilson observe (xiv), 'from the earliest work to the most recent, augers ill. Almost invariably the man regards the woman as an object, neglects, abuses, ill-treats and diminishes her . . . .' Joan Riley's novels suggest that the black male's own racial and economic victimization is partly responsible for his oppression of women, and some of Hazel Campbell's and Olive Senior's stories reveal the social and historical factors that sanction male tyranny in West Indian households. Erna Brodber's fiction is one of the few exceptions which suggests a more positive coexistence between the sexes is both possible and necessary.

Women in the texts are represented as valuing relational interaction in all fields, and the writers acknowledge the importance of female bonding and support. This is not to assert any easy affirmation of sisterhood; as noted, in the literature as in the society, several factors mitigate against female solidarity. However, in novels like *Crick Crack Monkey*, *Beka Lamb*, Beryl Gilroy's *Frangipani House* and Grace Nichols's *Whole of a Morning Sky,* protagonists draw a great deal of strength from their connections with other women, and in Chapter 4 I stress the communal orientation of the fiction.

Finally, West Indian women's writing emphasizes a sustaining affinity with native place and landscape – the works of Rhys, Allfrey and Brodber are cases in point – which can engender what Lorna Goodison (1990: 292–3) evocatively calls 'Heartease'. At times, the natural world is the gateway to the realm of spirits, the magical, that exists side-by-side with the everyday: Brodber's novels, *Annie John*, and several stories in Olive Senior's and Opal Palmer Adisa's collections demonstrate this juxtaposition.

And what about 'form'?

Davies and Fido's introduction to *Out of the Kumbla* defines the 'voicelessness' of women in the West Indian literary tradition as 'the historical absence of the woman writer's text: the absence of a specifically female position on major issues such as slavery, colonialism, decolonization, women's rights and more direct social and cultural issues' (I). From the above synopsis, we can safely state that this is no longer the case. But Davies and Fido also point to another 'voicelessness', a formal problem for all Caribbean writers, and perhaps doubly so for women: the difficulty of expressing their experience in the language of the oppressor. Women writers are aware of the difficulties of working in standard English, 'the master's tongue',[3] but see the range of linguistic options available within the creole continuum,[4] as well as the rich resources of the oral tradition, as positive creative challenges. Indeed, Mordecai and Wilson (ix) note 'the variety of forms and the special exhilaration which Caribbean women writers bring to the use of language.' Throughout this book, I will be mentioning examples of this linguistic variation.

The same goes for formal innovation: from the multiple narrative of *Wide Sargasso Sea* in 1966, to the surrealistic – or, perhaps, postmodern – fictions of Brodber and Kincaid (in the 1980s) which disregard distinctions between the realms of dream/spirit/empirical reality, the trend seems to be toward a rejection of the linear, realistic narrative. Perhaps this is in reaction to the realist nineteenth century English novel, until recently held up for admiration by the school system; certainly, the fact that my students were suspicious of texts that didn't conform to the 'beginning-middle-end' formula, demonstrates the pervasiveness of the tradition. Again, one can speculate – indeed, Brodber (1990) provides evidence – that the choice of an eclectic, fragmented structure (*Annie John, Jane and Louisa* and Velma Pollard's *Considering Woman* make use of a series of 'snapshots', assembled in apparently random order) is linked to the representation of complex psychological states produced by conflicting pressures on the female consciousness. Additionally, the easy blend of visual observation and exploration of interior states can be related to what Pat Ismond has called the particularly 'open consciousness' of the child, which many of these writers convincingly portray.

A related feature in the fiction of West Indian women, one they hold in common with Afro-American writers like Alice Walker, is the multiplicity of narrative voices/perspectives within a text. Stylistically, this facilitates the representation of a world of fluid boundaries' between self/other; living/dead; mad/sane; dream/reality. Carolyn Cooper (1991) alludes to this fluidity when she posits the use of the trope of spirit possession as metaphorical of the recovery of African cultural values in the black diaspora, and suggests that a revalorization of such 'discredited knowledge' – in the sense of the term as used by Toni Morrison (1985: 342) – is a major project in the female-centred fictions of Sylvia Wynter, Erna Brodber and Paule Marshall (the latter acknowledges the influence on her style of the multiple voices of women in her mother's kitchen!).[5] Reappropriation of what Cooper terms 'devalued folk wisdom – that body of subterranean knowledge that is often associated with the silenced language of women and the "primitiveness" of orally transmitted knowledge' (65) – is important to the recuperation of identity for the female in these works.

The communal focus of West Indian women's narrative, noted earlier, obviously suggests the importance of the oral tradition in the region and serves, as Nasta observes of post-colonial women writers (xx), to tell 'the story of a previously unwritten history and culture' from the female side. Davies and Fido (6) concur with this link in West Indian women's fiction between oral history and scribal 'collective story', noticing a 'thematic quilting' between stories: and indeed, the short story collection – by women like Senior, Kincaid, Campbell, McKenzie and the Sistren collective – is enjoying great popularity.

In terms of style, we also noted the richly allusive nature of the writing, which draws freely on Biblical narrative, proverb, songs (of all kinds), fairy tale and indigenous folk tale, with the latter requiring some revision given the essential misogyny of much West Indian oral culture (Thorpe, 1986; Davies, 1990: 185–7). Similarly, little respect is paid to traditional genre boundaries; narrative moves fluidly between literary styles (prosaic, parodic, dramatic, lyric, satiric) and techniques (reported speech, dialogue, 'stream of consciousness', monologue, fantasy and so on). There is a sense in which the writing refuses, to use Wilson Harris's term, 'consolidation' by any language, register or formal device.

While acknowledging this refusal to be bound by traditional forms, it can be said that West Indian women writers – in common with women writers worldwide – tend to use the 'autobiographical first person narrator'. This is not to say they simply write their personal lives but rather, as Betty Wilson is quoted in *Out of the Kumbla* (6),

> that the structure of the fictional autobiography, journal, diary, letter or other relatively 'intimate' genres seem to be the preferred vehicle for expressing feminine/feminist/female consciousness. The autobiographical form allows a sort of re-vision, a radical re-shaping of a life, seen and recounted from the inside. . . .

It is also the case that such 'confessional' or intimate narratives prove to be as much explorations of national and political as of personal concerns.[6] Hence, the maturing of the protagonist in *Beka Lamb* parallels the growth in political consciousness of Belize, and Annie John's disenchantment with the myopia of her colonized mother, in the eponymous novel, suggests Antigua's disenchantment with colonial ideology. The female protagonist's initiation into the complexities of the adult world reflects the development of a 'national' as well as a 'personal' identity. The conflated 'herstory' is indeed a collective one.

Finally, it should be said that West Indian women's fiction is inherently subversive, despite the general tendency to eschew strident political rhetoric. Many writers admit to a motivating desire for social change. They see race/class hierarchies as dehumanizing, and gender restrictions as stultifying; with Merle Hodge (1990: 208) they seem to admire 'women who [do] not know their place'. Accordingly, their works explore narrative avenues of resistance, from parodying patriarchal posturing (as illustrated in Chapter 5) to rewriting canonical works of empire (*Wide Sargasso Sea's* revision of *Jane Eyre*; *Annie John's* interrogation of *Paradise Lost*, as discussed in Chapter 3). Discovering the particular literary forms taken by the fusion of political commitment and creative praxis in West Indian women's fiction, considerably adds to the pleasure of reading their work.

Questions of definition

The texts mentioned above by no means cover the entire range of fiction by West Indian women; yet even in this small corpus, the striking variety – of concerns, subject matter, social visions, linguistic ranges, formal experiments – is apparent. Critics have certainly noticed this. Esteves and Paravisini-Gebert (xxvi) consider 'the most salient feature of the stories collected here is their presentation of the multiplicity of voices of Caribbean women'. Nasta explains that her collection of essays is informed by 'the sounds of a number of varied, dynamic and contesting voices which are currently speaking out and defining their plurality' (xxix). Davies and Fido (16) consider their editorial task incomplete, given the *wealth* of literary offerings by women.

Shelton (356) is struck by the wide range of preoccupations and responses of francophone women authors. Mordecai and Wilson (ix) complain about the difficulty of selecting for their anthology 'a final, tiny, sample' out of the variety on offer. Kathleen Balutansky (1990: 546), reviewing *Her True–True Name*, emphasizes the fact that 'Caribbean women – and their voices – tend to be as distinct from each other as are their countries, and as their various racial, social, economic and cultural positions would suggest.' And Greene (536) concludes that 'Caribbean women's writing defied easy definitions of any kind'.

At the same time, all these critics, by simply using a term like 'Caribbean women writers', implicitly or explicitly assume *something* unifies them as a group. What is this? The fact that they are *women*? If so, what distinguishes their literary productions from West Indian literature as a whole? It cannot be only a matter of the thematic and stylistic features generally embodied in their work, for, as was frequently pointed out to me in the process of teaching my course on this writing, *many* of the features listed above can be identified in West Indian texts by men. Just to cite obvious examples, Naipaul details states of extreme alienation; Lamming exposes the damaging effects of internalizing race and class hierarchies as normative; Selvon writes of the migration experience; and Harris employs fluid time, blurs boundaries of consciousness and character, and moves easily between dream and reality. This is natural, for as Shelton (346) reminds us, writing by Caribbean women *is* inscribed within the 'general discursive space' of the Caribbean literary tradition. Esteves and Paravisini-Gebert (xiii) expand on this:

> In their search for their individual voices as Caribbean writers, women have had to address the traditional themes and tropes of Caribbean literature – slavery, the plantation economy, colonialism, the complexities of class, race, and language – from their own particular vantage point, that of women from emerging nations where patriarchal/colonial institutions have sought to silence women's voices in general – and coloured women's voices in particular.

But Greene (533) makes a crucial point when she cites general agreement by writers and critics

> that Caribbean women have their own view of reality . . . [and] their literature is essentially different from that of Caribbean males (and of women outside the Caribbean) . . . [and] although race, class, identity and so on were commonalities, women experience all of these in a way different from the way men experienced them. In other words, all other categories were subsumed under gender.

Therefore, it seems that the 'particular vantage point' of West Indian women writers is a post-colonial feminist one, and I will return to this issue in Chapter 3.

Unfortunately, both these labels have connotations of a 'confrontational' stance, of revelling in 'Otherness' and if postmodernism has taught us anything, it is a healthy suspicion of binary oppositions. Hence, as Nasta (xvi) insists, it is counterproductive to consider the project of women writers from the Caribbean (and other non-Western territories) as merely 'redressing the balance; the[ir] reclamation [of a voice] is more than simply shifting the ground of a series of oppositions and areas of struggle: whether male/female, coloniser/native, black/white, feminist/womanist, post-colonial/post-structuralist, Third World/First World, traditional literary canons/counter-discourses and forms'. However, as long as the kind of oppositions mentioned above continue to inform the political reality of many women's lives in the region, it will be hard not to utilize them in speaking about women's writing. At the same time, I would agree with Nasta that any theoretical approach to the writing needs to go *beyond* the limited notion of a 'literature of opposition' set up by such dialectics 'and make space for the expression of a "multiplicity of perspectives" and literary poetics'. (xvi)

What *kind* of approach would this be, to be able to account for 'unity in diversity'? Obviously, a theory in the best creole tradition, as syncretic and inclusive as the women's literary voices it seeks to elucidate: a theory that I attempt to sketch in the next section.

Woman version

Two further critical comments may serve to preface the approach I have in mind. Esteves and Paravisini-Gebert (xiii) see Caribbean women's writing as both echoing *and* subverting the themes and tropes of regional literature, 'often calling into question accepted notions and well established "truths", revealing aspects of the Caribbean experience not previously gleaned from literary or historical accounts.' Balutansky (1990: 539) asserts that 'Caribbean women's writings are not mere sub/versions of Caribbean male narratives . . . [but] are autonomous and diverse expressions of a woman-centred Caribbean experience.' The essential idea here is of a discourse inextricably bound up with, yet growing out of, the West Indian 'master' discourse, emerging as one which moves beyond a subversive, interrogational relationship with the latter towards a distinct, self-directed envisioning that is both 'woman-centred' and diverse. Parallels can immediately be observed here with the way Creole languages come into being, and it is appropriately from creole culture that I draw the musical analogy – I hesitate to say 'paradigm' – that may help to conceptualize West Indian women's fiction as I see it.

In *Cut 'N' Mix: Culture, Identity and Caribbean Music*[7] Dick Hebdige conceives of the relationship between Caribbean music and cultural identity in dynamic terms. Accordingly, he sees the task of tracing and identifying sources and origins as futile; rather, his intention is to show 'how the roots themselves are in a state of constant flux and change' (10). There *is* no essential, definitive source as there is no one, definitive musical 'text', because in Caribbean music,

> [t]he collective voice is given precedence over the individual voice of the artist or the composer. Rhythm and percussion play a much more central role. In the end, there is a link in these non-European musics with public life, with speech, with the textures and the grain of the living human voice. (11)

This is certainly true of the 'version', a development of reggae music in Jamaica in the late 1960s, which Hebdige thinks is conceptually central to '*all* Afro-American and Caribbean musics: jazz, blues, rap, r & b, reggae, calypso, soca, salsa . . .' (12). Basically, the version is just that: a modification of a popular reggae record. *Hundreds* of different versions may follow the release of such a record, each slightly different from the original. Hebdige explains how:

> A musician will play a different solo on a different instrument, use a different tempo, key or chord sequence. A singer will place the emphasis on different words or add new ones. A record producer will use a different arrangement. An engineer will stretch the sounds into different shapes, add sound effects, take out notes and chords or add new ones, creating empty spaces by shuffling the sequence of sounds into new patterns. (12)

A collective enterprise indeed! The point is that in 'playing with' elements of the original – which remains 'recognizably there' on the dub – and adding new ones, something entirely new is created. And given sophisticated equipment, experimentation in dub is boundless, so that some producers have created 'music [that] is beginning to resemble modern, free-form jazz. The original tune is stretched, broken and bent into the most extraordinary shapes by all kinds of electronic wizardry.' (84)

In addition, by 1970 the 'dj talk over' added a new track on which a dj like the famous U Roy actually *speaks* over the rhythm. 'Talk over' is not a strictly accurate term: each dj has his own style. Hebdige describes U Roy as at times resembling 'the inspired ravings of a worshipper "trumping in the spirit" at a Pocomania gathering' (84);[8] others added 'snatches of song and nursery rhymes', jokes, 'sincere fatherly advice', and echoes of 'the old African boast songs' (85). Most drew heavily on Rastafarian imagery and idiom, and like Trinidadian calypsonians, utilized 'intertextual' references, alluding to, mocking and parodying their rivals' efforts.

Hebdige's account is fascinating, but my intention in mentioning it here has been simply to intimate the *complexity* of a form often dismissed by the uninitiated as 'sub/versions'. In fact, what Hebdige's discussion does is to call into question (13ff) the whole notion of a hierarchical distinction between original 'substantive creation' and the 'version', a new form that has grown out of a *process* of altering, supplementing, breaking, echoing, mocking and playing with that original.

To return to West Indian women's writing: what I suggest is that we approach this writing, in light of the above, as a kind of remix or dub version, which utilizes elements from the 'master tape' of Caribbean literary discourse (combining, stretching, modifying them in new ways); announces a gendered perspective; adds individual styles of 'talk over'; enhances or omits tracks depending on desired effect; and generally alters by recontextualization to create a *unique* literary entity. The charge that the dub version, like women's literature, always privileges the original (the male dominated canon) which it plays with/subverts, can be countered with the claim that the 'original' is itself but a selection from a plethora of tracks (potential meanings) laid down in the 'pre-version'. In recuperating what was always potentially there but excised in the 'cover version', the dub remix in fact refuses to privilege *any* version over others. Andrew Goodwin (34–39) notes postmodernist orientations in this impulse, as it informs more recent musical forms like 'sampling'.

Analogies between musical and literary 'scores' recur in discussions of Afro-American and Caribbean writing: both Henry Louis Gates, Jr. (1987) and Houston Baker, Jr. (1984) use 'blues criticism' in analyzing Afro-American literature, and Edward Brathwaite (1967–8) discusses Roger Mais's *Brother Man* as a 'jazz novel'. The title of Toni Morrison's *Jazz* (1992) explicitly embodies this impulse. In the following chapters I attempt to use general correspondence between the dub version and the literary 'woman version' to suggest theoretical guidelines for reading West Indian women's fiction. At one level the literature can be described as accessing the 'flip side' of Caribbean discourse, articulating an alternative perspective on/reaction to/ subversion of issues of race, class, gender and identity as they have been consolidated in mainstream Caribbean literature. Formally, attention to 'd(o)ubleness' uncovers an interweaving – for example, of speech codes, as Pollard (1991: 248) discovers in the work of Lorna Goodison:

> [t]he rendering of complex behaviours and the sound of complex voices in a single statement by the deft manipulation of lexicon and syntax of the different codes. . . .

Using the analogy of the dub version, the informed reader can discover in West Indian women's texts 'a multiple consciousness in what seems on the surface to be a single mode of expression' (Pollard, 1991: 251).

Chapter summaries

The main part of this book tests the efficacy of various critical and theoretical practices (which I deliberately cannibalize and 'mix') in elucidating the 'woman version' of West Indian literature, particularly as they share with the fiction an attention to syncretism, multiplicity, adaptability, open-endedness and a refusal of consolidation.

One aspect of the concept of the 'woman version' is its transcendence of the kind of limited dialectical model which Nasta warns against, one which focuses on the tension between opposed factions (colonizer/colonized, male/female, black/white). Instead, attention is paid to the 'loosening up' of static confrontational models of representation. This consideration informs Chapter 1.

As noted, attempts to determine the roots of the version are far less useful than attending to the dynamic of *interrelating* sources and influences. Now, in the West Indies, the feminist project of discovering a female tradition, establishing literary foremothers/ 'a literature of their own'[9] for contemporary women writers, has been made problematic. Although there does exist a body of narratives written by women from and about the region since at least the nineteenth century, the fact that these early texts were almost invariably written by expatriates or 'white' creoles has tended to give rise to prescriptive injunctions as to their 'relevance', given the marginal value of their perspectives *vis-à-vis* the experience of the majority of (non-white) West Indian women. However, using the tactics of the 'woman version' – undermining the confrontational model of difference that underlies such comments, and exploring the interrelationship of sources and influences – the articulations of the other 'colonizing subject' and the white creole 'outsider' are given a hearing. Since, like the dub version, women's writing makes a political point of incorporating the marginal, the peripheral, the apparently irrelevant, such early narratives shed light on the variety of female experience, including that of silenced black women, in the region.

Chapter 2 seeks to apply another traditional feminist literary approach – a focus on 'images of woman' – to West Indian women's fiction which, like the dub version, explores discordance. Like jazz music, the dub version breaks, twists, bends and stretches traditional elements into apparently bizarre new forms. As has been pointed out, there is no *one* authentic West Indian identity, much less a definitive female one; rather, as the chapter demonstrates, images of Caribbean womanhood have been constructed in various ways, since slavery, for specific discursive purposes. The internalization of several such images informs female socialization in the region, and can have disastrous effects on the female psyche, especially that of the black woman.

Accordingly, the phenomenon of texts by women which represent 'mad' protagonists – those whose alienation is so severe as to put them outside West Indian concepts of normalcy – is examined here. It can be argued that such texts demonstrate both the pernicious influence of certain stereotypes and the inadequacy of available models, *and* represent their radical deconstruction via an 'opting out' of *all* models/roles/images of womanhood by the 'mad' characters. Paradoxically, the choice of an often self-destructive option signifies a survival strategy in the woman's search for self-definition. Again, these extreme articulations of female 'Otherness' suggest a disquieting 'woman version' of portrayals of the female in West Indian literature, and reinforce Merle Hodge's claim (1990: 202) for 'the power of the creative word to change the world'.

In Chapter 3 the important contribution of post-colonial theory is examined with reference to West Indian women's fiction. Post-colonial theory focuses on power relations between imperial centre and marginal colony, situating the emergence of post-colonial literatures within this experience. Such literatures foreground 'their differences from the assumptions of the imperial centre',[10] subverting and transforming imperial language in this 'resistance struggle'. In seeking ultimately to dismantle the centre/margin paradigm that informs colonial ideology, post-colonial theory has parallels with the dub version which, as I have explained, disturbs notions of a privileged, original 'substantive' creation (the master narrative) and a marginalized, inferior copy version. Instead, the 'original' becomes public property, part of the material which different artists rewrite/recreate for their own purposes.

Since imperial discourse constitutes woman and native in similar ways, and both are linked with 'virgin' territories to be raped and colonized, post-colonial and feminist theory overlap in their interrogation of what Lemuel Johnson, discussing Michelle Cliff's work (132), calls 'histories of racial and gender misrepresentation'. At the same time, post-colonial theory has been criticized for homogenizing 'native' cultures and for ignoring internal divisions within these cultures: conflicts which include those of gender, race and class.

In this chapter, women writers who challenge imperial and patriarchal assumptions, often through subversive manipulation of genre and the Creole continuum, are considered; and so are divisions *within* post-colonial society in the West Indies (divisions signalled by intersecting/competing language varieties) as they affect women. A healing option is exploitation of a sensibility of 'd(o)ubleness', symbolized by protagonists who refuse to be trapped by imposed choices of gender role, language and class allegiance.

As noted, no one 'woman version' or vision claims to be definitive; each reveals only a partial truth in that other 'deferred' versions also exist, even potentially. Factors such as the writer's socio-cultural position within Caribbean discourse, her gender and political orientation constitute authorial 'talk over' and stamp an individual mark on her version. Yet, as Hebdige demonstrates with reference to U Roy and his immediate successors, the 'dj talk over' is *itself* drawn from a collective cultural discourse (specifically, an afrocentric, creole folk culture). Thus the dub version in effect problematizes the whole concept of subjectivity as constituted by imperial and patriarchal discourse, particularly the notion of the 'individual' subject with a single voice and agenda.

Accordingly, in Chapter 4, textual exposure of the methods by which colonized woman was 'written out' of subjectivity, becoming a 'zombi' in imperial discourse, develops into a discussion of whether the female writer can recuperate a female West Indian subject within such an inherited tradition. In the female-authored text, a corrective possibility is explored: a 'collective subjectivity' in its *relational*, as opposed to egocentrically oppositional, manifestation, more suited to the concept of the 'woman version'.

In Chapter 5 the propensity of the dub/'woman version' for allusion, as well as parody and travesty, is considered as part of a transformative strategy. These tendencies are reviewed in the light of Bakhtin's concept of the 'carnivalesque' in the novel as a comic subversion of dogma, and Irigaray's suggestion that mimicry of phallocentric discourse is in fact a political act. The effect in all cases is at least an interrogation, if not a turning on its head, of the old hierarchical order which marginalizes the female. By irreverently mocking and parodying West Indian assumptions about authority and respectability (based as these are on norms of, inevitably male, power), certain texts by women are shown to indict the foundations of patriarchal authority which exist at the expense of a communally oriented, nurturing social ethos more privileged in female fictions.

Chapter 6 attempts to review the main orientations of the 'woman version' and the theoretical approaches that best elucidate its complexity, variety, inclusiveness, indeterminacy and syncretism. Eclecticism is not only permitted, but advocated, with certain strictures, and a consideration of the *intersection* of ideological and formal priorities is seen to be crucial to any study of West Indian women's fiction.

Understandably, many of the writers (and scholars) of this literature distrust 'theory' and its tendency to appropriate and subsume marginal texts. Theoretical rigidity and orthodoxy are anathema to a fictional discourse that embraces pluralities and to which complexity is fundamental. Taking my cue from the writers themselves, therefore, I do not attempt to construct a single theoretical model for West Indian women's writing but, rather, to suggest the need for plural and syncretic theoretical approaches which can take account of the multiplicity, complexity, the intersection of apparently conflicting orientations which we find in the writing: approaches which can combine heterogeneity *and* commonality while refusing to be ultimately formalized under any one 'ism'. This chapter argues that no one critical/theoretical position is adequate to deal with West Indian fictions by women, and suggests instead an 'aesthetic of pluralism' as most efficacious in literary and political terms. In other words the writing is theoretically situated within the creole ethos from which it arises.

Woman Version is a beginning. I haven't attempted a comprehensive overview of West Indian writing by women *or* of critical responses to and debates about the literature. Neither have I compared fictions by male writers with those by women, in any systematic way. I suggest, rather than prescribe, how the fictions might be read, and encourage overlapping (with the inevitable repetition involved) of theoretical positions. Because of these omissions, I anticipate what Susheila Nasta terms 'dissenting voices'; but these will also serve the purpose of opening up the texts to more sensitive and multilayered readings. For in the end, my intention – and that of *all* studies of West Indian women's writing – is to bring to public awareness and appreciation, a body of literature that articulates, with spirit and feeling and wit, what it means to be a woman in this wonderful region.

Notes

1   The term 'West Indian' is somewhat problematic, given that it is a misnomer and inscribes the region within the terms of Columbus's ignorance, but I use it throughout to indicate the geographic and linguistic specificity of the literature under discussion.

2   A sample of the better known anthologies of Caribbean/West Indian fiction reveals greater or lesser degrees of marginalization of women writers; in all cases, the majority of inclusions are male-authored. Andrew Salkey's *West Indian Stories* (1960) contains 25 stories, none by women; Kenneth Ramchand's *Best West Indian Stories* (1982) has three stories by women in a collection of 20; Mervyn Morris's *Contemporary Caribbean Short Stories* (1990) includes 24 stories of which five are female authored; and Stewart Brown's *Caribbean New Wave: Contemporary Caribbean Short Stories* (1990) tops the list with nine of the 23 pieces written by women.

3   See Marlene Nourbese Philip, Michelle Cliff, Grace Nichols, Merle Hodge and Jean D'Costa in Cudjoe (ed.) (1990) and, briefly, Olive Senior (1988: 482).

4   For a definition of the concept of the Creole continuum, see Pollard (1991: 239–40); it is also discussed in Chapter 3.

5   See Paule Marshall (1983: 3–12).

6   Cudjoe (1985) and Morrison (1985) note the importance of autobiography in African-American literature as the 'autobiography of the tribe' where, as Cudjoe puts it 'the concerns of the collective predominate. One's personal experiences are assumed to be an authentic expression of the society. . . .' (10).

7   I am indebted to Mike Alleyne, talented student and musician, for bringing this book to my attention and for helping to refine my layman's understanding of the complex process of musical production.

8   As the *Dictionary of Jamaican English* (Cassidy and LePage, 1980: 56) explains, Pocomania is a creolized Jamaican cult 'mixing revivalism with ancestral-spirit possession'.

9   The term is, of course, from the title of Elaine Showalter's groundbreaking study of British women novelists (1977).

10   Ashcroft, Griffiths and Tiffin (1989: 2).

CHAPTER 1

Early versions: outsiders' voices/ silenced voices

The point has been made by now that West Indian women's writing did not 'emerge' fully-formed in the 1970s, and there is growing interest in recuperating texts by early writers whose work, it turns out, problematizes certain assumptions made about primary interculturation in the region and re-evaluates fixed roles historians and literary critics have tended to ascribe to race and gender groups during and after slavery. In this chapter, I argue that the ambivalent space occupied by many of the early women writers within the West Indian literary tradition provides a unique point of departure for deconstructing some of the informing myths of colonialism and national identity.

Who were they? Brenda Berrian's *Bibliography of Women Writers from the Caribbean* (1989: x) cites the *History* (1831) of Mary Prince, a Bermudan slave, as the earliest female-authored work of prose in the region, although, with other slave narratives, the question of her authorship of the text has been raised. Subsequently, according to Berrian (x) the 'four earliest known women writers' were Jamaicans: Mary Seacole, Pamela C. Smith, Clarine Stephenson and Mary F. Lockett. Seacole's 'autobiographical travelogue' was published in 1857; Smith's collection of folklore (1899) was followed by Lockett's novel *Christopher* in 1902; Stephenson published a poem in the 1909 edition of the *Jamaica Times*, and a novel, *Undine*, in 1911.

There were others, of course. For example, I have managed to collect some of Mrs Henry Lynch's prolific nineteenth century output on Jamaica, and Jamaican Henrietta Jenkin's *Cousin Stella* (1859), as well as Frieda Cassin's Antiguan novel, *With Silent Tread* (c. 1896), predate both Lockett and Stephenson's texts. In the field of travel writing, journals and collections of letters, there is a wealth of narrative material from the region prior to 1900. But if the work of 'lady novelists' received little serious attention until recently, travel narratives and the like were accorded even less status within traditional literary studies. Considered as 'typically feminine' vehicles for women at a literary loose end, or rather suspect sources of socio-historical data, such writings have been largely ignored in West Indian academic circles.

In the early twentieth century too, despite scant attention paid to the fact, women writers like Elma Napier and Jean Rhys from Dominica, and Eliot Bliss and Alice Durie of Jamaica, were publishing fiction in the 1930s. By the 1950s, according to Berrian, the list had grown to include, among others, Phyllis Shand Allfrey (Dominica), Ada Quayle, Vera Bell and Cicely Waite-Smith (writing on Jamaica), and Celeste Dolphin (Guyana).

Now, feminist literary theory has long stressed the importance of tracing 'literary foremothers', and recovering forgotten works by writers who helped to establish a 'female tradition' within regional literatures. This project is especially urgent in the West Indies where metropolitan publishers have not seen fit to reprint most of the material, and local libraries are either unable to or uninterested in preserving it properly: Bernadette Farquhar (33) in her review of *With Silent Tread* mentions that the copy she read, possibly the only one in the region, was found in a dustbin outside the public library in Antigua. Additionally, one can read much into the fact that to consult most of the pre-twentieth century West Indian texts, I had to travel to the copyright libraries of Britain!

In terms of critical attention, Seacole's reprinted (1984) autobiography has received critical analysis locally from Christine Craig and, more recently, Evelyn Hawthorne. Importantly, Craig (33–4) links Seacole's text with those of other women from the region (or, in the case of Lady Nugent, women resident for some time in, and writing about, the West Indies) who treat of the problematic figure of the creole woman. The term – as used by Nugent and Rhys – refers to local-born *whites*, although much has been made of Rhys's creole woman in *Wide Sargasso Sea* as racially mixed, and indeed, this is what Seacole means by 'creole'. Craig thinks such texts provide 'valuable insight into the values and mores of a creole woman. . . [one] visibly neither black nor white, who could, therefore, to some extent, experience both worlds' (34).

Craig and Hawthorne highlight the cultural ambivalence of the creole woman, drawn to the metropole while rooted in the Caribbean, an ambivalence shared by most colonials but one which the creole woman geographically acts out in the text. Seacole (55) claims that 'I . . . have good Scotch blood coursing in my veins' *and* that she is one of the 'hot-blooded creoles' of Jamaica (59). Hence, the editors of the 1984 edition observe (39) that in Mrs Seacole

> and in her writing are combined the conflicting elements of pride in her African ancestry and unquestioning acceptance of British culture and attitudes, which sometimes manifested itself in her use of pejorative European terminology [such as 'nigger'].

This dual loyalty was further complicated by Seacole's personal experience of racism when, in the course of her travels to the Crimea, she arrived in London.

Importantly, Hawthorne calls attention to the ways in which Seacole's somewhat exceptional choice of genre – the travel narrative was largely the province of the bourgeois male adventurer – undercuts the conventions associated with this patriarchal form, while observing that her autobiographical input self-consciously complicated that Victorian ideal of femininity enshrined in nineteenth century fiction. As Cudjoe (1990: 13) notes, Seacole 'broke out of the traditional roles assigned to women at the time' by voluntarily travelling alone, practising medicine, and setting up in business; in addition, of course, she wrote her own life. Hawthorne argues that Seacole's self-representation, with its emphasis on her industry, her Caribbean-sanctioned self-reliance, and her achievements despite the odds, is an implicit vindication of the creole woman who, as we shall see, was a frequent target for accusations of sloth and immorality.

The features pointed out by these critics – the uneasy middle ground between black and white occupied by the creole, ambivalent relations with 'Mother Country' and motherland, the engagement with European 'feminine' ideals, and the necessity for creating a narrative space from which to speak – inform other early works and are fundamental to any concept of a 'woman version' on West Indian literature. But the fact that, apart from Prince and Seacole, nearly all the other writers mentioned were white, undoubtedly complicates the project of 'reclaiming' their work. *Black* women, on the other hand, were for the most part silent, in literary terms, until well into the twentieth century, due to restrictions of social, educational and economic circumstances. Of course, there *were* literate black women during slavery and after,[1] and the possibility exists that some wrote autobiography, poetry or fiction, but as far as I have been able to ascertain, nothing has been preserved. Given the politics of publishing in the West Indies then (as now), it is unlikely that anything saw print that did not serve the missionary/ abolitionist cause, and of this, the little that survives is in verse. Carolyn Cooper (1991) discusses one exceptional song/poem recorded around 1793 that articulates a black slave woman's sexual exploitation, and her refusal to accept white moral censure.[2] But, it seems, to have access to the earlier prose 'woman versions' we must attend to the 'outsider's' voice.

For indeed, this is how early white women writers have been perceived. One of the first critics to write comprehensively on the West Indian novel, Kenneth Ramchand (1972: 225) initially argued for the inclusion of texts by white West Indians in the literary canon, because of their 'social relevance': that is, their portrayal of the 'terrified consciousness' of elites in the decolonization process. However, he does note that such writers 'tended to be neglected in the demanding contexts of Black nationalism', which in the 1950s and 1960s was naturally concerned with redressing the balance of centuries of British colonial exploitation and its concomitant racism. And, it must be remembered, West Indian literature came into its own and shared the political goals of the various popular political movements toward independence. Therefore it is hardly surprising, given this context, that he comes to consider the literature as an essentially twentieth century phenomenon and argues (1988: 95) of the earlier narratives that when literature from the region

> was not the production of planters and planter-types, government officials, visitors, missionaries, and other birds of passage writing from alien perspectives, it was the writing of a small group or class either pursuing its own narrow interests or committed to the idea of Europe as home and center.

Several of the writers I have mentioned *are* indeed related to those waved aside: they were obviously not 'government officials', but their wives and daughters; not 'planters or planter-types' (whatever the latter might be), but their female dependants; visitors, certainly, but visitors who settled and often married into West Indian society; and, since they were white, they did, generally speaking, belong to 'a small group or class' that had an often romanticized 'idea of Europe as home and center'. However, given the wide range of class allegiances in the group Ramchand refers to, 'caste' might be a better term.

Does this disqualify their writing as West Indian, and if so, why? Gareth Griffiths (1987: 13) considers the problem with 'first texts produced in a post-colonial society' to be their representation 'of the viewpoint of the colonising centre' since the writers – 'gentrified settlers, administrators . . . travellers, sightseers . . .' – appear 'to have been born hand in hand with the Imperial enterprise'. Such writing, he feels, is dominated by the oppressive influence of imperial language and culture, and is thus implicated in the colonizing project. In other words, its politics are offensive from a contemporary post-colonial perspective.

For Edward Kamau Brathwaite, race is the crucial factor. 'There are of course, "white people" in the West Indies,' he admits (1963: 16), 'but these are regarded either as too far apart to count or too inextricably mixed into the whole problem to be considered as separate.' Despite the difficulty pointed out by Edward Baugh (1981: 113) of adequately summarizing Brathwaite's views, given his prolific critical output over the last 30 or so years, Baugh thinks (112) that Brathwaite has been fairly consistent in positing 'the folk', 'the broadly ex-African base' (1969: 270) as the matrix of Caribbean culture and art. Logically then, white writers – those who have been 'inextricably mixed' are no longer a separate entity – represent the 'outsider's voice' and have nothing to say of relevance to a West Indian literary tradition. This appears to be Brathwaite's conclusion in *Contradictory Omens* (1974: 38), where his analysis of the integration of other groups into the Afro-Caribbean 'norm and model' reveals that

> White creoles in the English and French West Indies have separated themselves by too wide a gulf, and have contributed too little culturally, as a *group*, to give credence to the notion that they can, given the present structure, meaningfully identify or be identified with the spiritual world on this side of the Sargasso Sea.

As I understand it, his argument is that the historical *facts* of white colonialism raised insurmountable ideological barriers between white West Indians (including writers) and the cultural mainstream, thus making it impossible for texts like *Wide Sargasso Sea* to constitute a truthful 'recognition of the realities of the situation': in other words, the white writer's perception and representation of experience does not relate to, nor is it relevant for, that of the non-white majority.

The trouble is, we are dealing with a disparate group of writers and to specify racial or political, or indeed class,[3] criteria for 'belonging' to West Indian literature, inevitably leads to more and more prescriptive injunctions about who is 'in' and who is 'out'. In the model of the dub version I posited earlier, the focus is less on the identification of one root source than on the *interrelationship* of influences. Paradoxically, it is Brathwaite who also argues that creolization involved creativity as well as imitative acculturation, and opposes the view of Caribbean culture as a static plural entity in favour of a vision of productive friction. In literature too, he reasons, a 'meaningful federation of cultures' is to be the goal. '[T]here will be no "one West Indian voice"' in West Indian literature, he declares (1969: 270), 'because there *is* no "one West Indian voice"' (italics mine).

I am in agreement here, and I want to argue for a theoretical stance that permits the inclusion of the 'outsider's voice' in any account of West Indian fiction by women. What we *make* of their articulations depends on a wide variety of factors.

Relevance of early narratives

To be practical, however, one must ask whether these early narratives, representing as they often do the voice of the colonizer's 'Other half', have any relevance for contemporary readers of West Indian women's writing? An obvious response is that it was largely *in reaction* to such colonial discourse that early 'mainstream' literature in the West Indies came to be written, and out of *this* mainstream comes the 'woman version'. There is certainly a thread of intertextual connection here. Another suggestion is that it is useful to read texts from the colonial period from a particular gender perspective in order to see how patriarchy in the imperial project was structured.

Again, David Trotter (3) notes that 'the academic study of colonialism. . . . has become the study of the roles allotted by the colonisers to the colonised: "representations of the colonial subject".' Critics like Homi Bhabha, Abdul JanMohammed and Gayatri Spivak, he maintains, who speak about 'the colonial subject',

> mean the *colonised* subject only. In their view, colonialism is an encounter between a colonising machine or system, on one hand, and a colonised subject, on the other. The *colonising* subject has been elided, his or her subjectivity wished away.

So texts that do provide access to 'the colonising subject' – particularly, in this case, the female of the species – may be usefully read for greater understanding of the 'master narrative' of empire that reverberated through West Indian literature, in one way or another, for so long.

But for European *women*, colonialism was essentially problematic. As Peterson and Rutherford (9) remind us, the colonial world

> was a man's world, demanding pioneering, martial and organisational skills, and the achievements of those in the shape of conquered lands and people were celebrated in a series of male-orientated myths. . . . At a later stage the same skills were used to overthrow colonialism, thus reinforcing the ethos of the colonies as a predominantly male domain, both in reality and in the popular imagination which was both formed by the myths and in turn shaped reality.

For the *female* 'colonising subject', there was precious little space in the popular imagination, nor the literature it produced. In a sense then, the concept of a 'female colonising subject' is a contradiction in terms, given that implementation of the colonizing project was 'officially' male. I am grateful to Jane Bryce for pointing out that the white woman writer of the colonial period can thus be seen as anomalous, inconvenient to the neat binary pigeon-holing of imperialism, and her writing significant precisely for this reason. The strategies of white women writers for inserting themselves into the history of colonization in the region, and thus into 'the popular imagination', are therefore all the more important to any study of the 'emergence' of West Indian literature by women.

A few examples of the early narratives by women will have to suffice. I read them first, for their (unwitting?) articulations of cracks in the edifice of the plantation system. Repeatedly, women writers point to the moral decay inherent in a society based on slavery. Eliza Fenwick, an English novelist, writing from Barbados to fellow-author Mary Hays – Fenwick lived in Barbados from 1814 to 1822 – confesses her fears regarding her son, Orlando, that 'the practices of severity, which are really essential in the government of Negroes, may chill and close his heart against those general sympathies which appear to me essential to the excellence of character' (1927 edition: 169–70). Lady Nugent, in her *Journal of her residence in Jamaica from 1801 to 1805*, also bemoans 'the immediate effect that the climate and habit of living in this country have upon the minds and manners of Europeans, particularly of the lower orders' (1966 edition: 98). Creole vices of sloth, over-indulgence, tyranny and 'the influence of the black and yellow women' (12) are soon acquired by white men – from Scottish overseer (29), to English soldier (172–3) to Lord Balcarres himself (38).

Fenwick's observation that in Barbados, white women live to a ripe old age but 'men shorten their period by intemperance and sensuality' (171), is echoed in several early narratives which evoke an overwhelming sense of the West Indies as a place of disease and death. Fenwick's son dies horribly and a litany of sudden deaths runs through Nugent's journal, although Mrs Carmichael's account of her stay in the West Indies in the early nineteenth century suggests that the psychological factor, the construction of the islands as lethal to whites, is also important: '[t]he greater number of people who die in the West Indies, die from apprehension' (1969 edition, Vol. 2: 314). The dark stain of slavery inevitably corrupts the white character in these accounts, unleashing vices that ultimately bring about decomposition (physically, morally, socially); a trope for the inherent deathliness of a plantation economy. The irony is clear to *us* in Fenwick's awareness that '[w]e who seek for gain in these climates have terrible penalties awaiting us' (196).

Interculturation also complicated the racial dichotomy implicit in the imperial project, and the degenerative effect on whites is cause for comment. As noted, Nugent views white creoles as irreversibly tainted by their association with blacks, their faces 'yellow [and] wrinkled' (10) and their language a 'tiresome' creole drawl. Carmichael observes that lower-class white men 'get a negro [woman] . . . to live with them, until they . . . become as the expression is, almost *a white negro*' (Vol 1: 59). Like Nugent (259), Mrs Henry Lynch, in her novel 'for young people' (1847: 17–18), acknowledges the thorough socialization of white creole children into the culture of black servants, evident in the material reality of language

> although my mother had taken pains to keep me from what is called, amongst West Indians, 'talking negro', yet, there was a langour and drawl in my manner of speaking, which drew from her the most cutting sarcasms.

Again, Hilary Beckles (forthcoming: 22) cites a contemporary source on the close association of 'poor-white' female hucksters with their black counterparts resulting in the white women carrying baskets on their heads and children strapped to their hips in the traditional African manner. Further, he notes, it was among working-class white women that association with slaves led to domestic/family liaisons with black and coloured men into the eighteenth century.

That such interculturation led inevitably to divided loyalties on the part of white creoles, is clear in Nugent's early nineteenth century allusion to simmering tensions between expatriate and local whites, the latter being quick to take offence at disparaging comments about themselves and vicious in their response. For example, after careful investigation, the creole ladies discover and publish abroad the 'common' background of an Englishwoman who gave offence in her talk of the 'natives' (202–3). Ethel Symonett's odd little novella (1895), a travel story of sorts, unmercifully mocks pejorative English prejudices about Jamaica and lauds the land and its people. There is a patriotism in her work, as in Lynch's earlier novel *Years Ago* (1865) – for example, a Jamaican education is seen to be the equal of an English one (40) – which complicates the notion of England as 'home' for these supposed daughters of empire.

Besides attending to an awareness of inconsistencies – both Nugent (140) and Carmichael (Vol 2: 250) complain of the uselessness of English schoolbooks for teaching West Indian children, a theme discussed in Chapter 3 – these early narratives can be read as accounts of the gendering of racism. Here, Hazel Carby's argument (1989, especially Chapter 2) is particularly useful. What she maintains is that 'two very different but interdependent codes of sexuality' operated in the American colonies, 'producing opposing definitions of motherhood and womanhood for white and black women which coalesce in the figures of the slave and the mistress' (20). Within the dominant discourse, white female sexuality was constructed in relation to the 'cult of true womanhood', with its feminine attributes of piety, sexual purity, submissiveness and domesticity (23). The fact that most white women's *material* reality was not a living embodiment of 'true womanhood' hardly mitigated the power of the stereotype. Indeed, Nugent's practice of riding on horseback, with her habit and 'short cropped head' (68), Fenwick's determined struggle to run a business virtually singlehanded, and Carmichael's account of the 'arduous' lives of drudgery led by planter's wives (Vol 1: 21–3), hardly conform to the vaporous stereotype.

Of course, stereotyping of any kind is inherently oppressive, but Carby's point (24–25) is that planter-class sexism and stereotyping had different consequences for white and black women, primarily because white women gave birth to heirs of property while black women gave birth to property, under slavery. Therefore the black woman came to be held up as the white woman's negative, her 'Other'. For example, the early narratives are reticent about white women's sexuality because, according to the stereotype, they had no such fleshly urges. By contrast, the 'black and yellow [mulatto] women' are stereotyped as wanton. Carmichael considers them 'peculiarly inclined to immorality' (Vol 1: 74), since 'to allure young men who are newly come to the country, or entice the inexperienced, may be said to be their principal object' (Vol 1: 71). Indeed, the heroine of Gabrielle Long's novel, *The Golden Violet,* quickly loses her husband to the sensual charms of a mulatto in pre-abolition Jamaica.

Similarly, given the importance of physical beauty as a reflection of inner beauty within the 'cult of true womanhood', black women in the female-authored narratives are inevitably judged as 'very ugly things to look upon': thus observes the heroine of Anne Marsh Caldwell's (1850) novel. However, Beckles (forthcoming: 15) cites contemporary accounts which suggest that white *men* in the Caribbean preferred brown-skinned black women to whites for sexual 'adventurism'. Gender and race inform contradictory evaluations throughout. As Carby (25) observes, what was considered a positive feature in black women ('strength and ability to bear fatigue'), was not proper to the white woman, with her delicate constitution.

Black women then, represented the 'alterity' of white femaleness. As Carby puts it (30), '[e]xisting outside the definition of true womanhood, black female sexuality was nevertheless used to define what those boundaries were.' So, while *all* women were constructed within this ideology in terms of restrictive stereotyping, female solidarity was not an issue because of the privileging of the racial factor.

Behind racism often lay the profit motive. Beckles (forthcoming: 7) stresses that specific economic factors underlay the elevation of the white woman as a model of chastity. When white women gave birth to the child of an enslaved (or free) black man, as did happen in the earlier slavery period, that child was legally free. Therefore to restrict the number of 'free coloureds', white men had to strictly limit the sexual freedom of white women, while continuing to exploit black women sexually as a 'normal benefit' of power *and* as sources of new labour.

Again, Beckles refers to unmarried or non-plantation white women in parts of the West Indies seeking to make a living in whatever niche was left by propertied white men in the market place – slave rental services, taverns, brothels and so on. And many used slaves toward such ends, particularly in urban centres, living by hiring out their property. So in Barbados in 1817, white women represented 50 per cent of those who owned properties stocked with less than 10 slaves (Beckles: 8) although the large slave holdings were virtually all male owned. And – so much for sisterhood – white women tended to own more female than male slaves. Beckles concludes (27) that this generally overlooked image of white women as slave owners mitigates against the perception of their anti-slavery sentiments or their shared victim-status under patriarchal oppression. Thus while the early narratives *are* often sensitively aware of slavery as a brutal system, sometimes ironically acknowledging a shared oppression by women and slaves under this system (Fenwick: 191: 'no slave that digs the field under a strict driver ever felt more fatigue and lassitude than I do when school closes'), their authors consistently align themselves with the source of power (white men) that was, at the same time, the source of their material and ideological marginalization.

Accordingly, as Carby notes, women 'were not only the subjects but also the perpetrators of oppression' (18). Nowhere is this seen more clearly in the early narratives than in their depictions of mistress/servant relations. Carby (37) notes of Mary Prince's story that while 'certain sympathies and similarities could exist between a white woman and her black female slave', both brutalized by men, the narrative reveals an awareness of the essential *difference* which white womanhood perceives in the black Other.

Any challenges to the confining strictures of 'true womanhood' by white women writers, she concludes, 'applied only to the white female characters' (33). It is to *black* women writers that Carby suggests we turn for a subversion of the conventions of this ideology, a challenge to its implicit racism and sexism; and indeed, this suggests a useful way of reading Seacole's *Wonderful Adventures*. But I would suggest that it *is* possible to read these early narratives as partially deconstructing the concept of the black woman as powerless and inferior.

For example, Fenwick, Nugent and Carmichael all complain of the 'turmoil and vexation' they face in the management of female slaves and servants, a crucial part of the white woman's role in the colonizing process. They repeatedly allude to the defiance, stubborn laziness, intractable deceit and thievery of these servants.[4] Here in the home, and often in the Great House (itself a symbol of hierarchical privilege in the plantation system), power relations begin to shift. For whatever they felt about black women, white women's lives were concerned with and *dependent* upon them to a great extent, which black women were aware of, and exploited – sometimes vindictively (Carmichael, Vol 2: 103–104).

As Beckles comments (1989, 68) the emotional crux of the matter involved the 'suckling, weaning and the socialization of their owner's children' by black or coloured domestics. For all their superior, instructive roles *vis-à-vis* servants, the mistresses relinquished power to some extent in handing over responsibility for their precious children. Nugent's wet nurse is white, yet she is a target of resentment for 'superseding me in one of the most precious parts of my expected duty' (122); usually the wet nurse was black.[5] In general then, when a female servant was commodified or 'appropriated for the children', as Carmichael (Vol 1: 29) puts it, 'she had twice the authority of either parent'. Further, she cites cases where the 'affection of the children towards . . . negro domestics was unbounded, and where they took no pains to conceal that they preferred the society of these servants to that of any white person'.

On the domestic front, then, enforced interaction and mutual dependency of black and white women suggests a destabilization of assumed hierarchical relations. Beckles (1989: 69) observes that:

> the unfolding of this complicated emotional and psychological entanglement presented slave holders with much discomfort. Many lived with the fear that nannies would murder their children, and as a result, infant mortalities were commonly enveloped in suspicion of foul play. Poisonings were rarely detected by white doctors. . . . When in 1774, for example, a slave nanny described by her owners as a 'favourite' was convicted of poisoning their infant, it was discovered that this was not the only occasion on which she had done so.

Acts of resistance, of subversion, as innocuous as a deliberate refusal to invest energy ('laziness') or as desperate as infanticide necessarily mitigate against the depiction of black women as powerless and passive. In these early narratives, 'silenced' black and mulatto women are a formidable presence. They constantly intrude into the personal and domestic lives of white women (areas with which the equivalent male texts are unfamiliar). The very constitution of the white female, her self-representation as 'mother' and 'wife' – note Bush's comment (44, 114) that white women were said to react with jealousy when white men sought out black women, and Cooper's (1991: 14) observation of the mistresses' fury when the slave woman bears a 'white' child, presumably for 'Massa' – is bound up with the complicating factor of the black woman's *participation* in these roles. In a sense, she both makes possible the existence of the 'ideal white woman' *and* exposes ambivalences within the ideology that gave rise to such a myth.

Finally, a useful insight into the unacknowledged significance of these early writings can be gained by approaching them as re-writings of the travel/adventure tale. Conventionally a male vehicle, with a quixotic hero setting out to brave the New World and make his fortune, the traveller's tale is of special importance in the West Indies. The narratives of Symonett and Fenwick, the fiction of Jenkin and Long follow a rather different pattern. Here we have European women with some degree of connection, by way of family, job or marriage, to the West Indies, setting off for this New World not to conquer but to *reintegrate* themselves.

The texts put forward 'versions' of the Caribbean already inscribed in colonial discourse – both positive and negative – to which the protagonists relate in a very personal way. Long's particularly nasty heroine anticipates playing the role of 'ministering angel amongst grateful savages' (21). Inevitably, expectations are shattered – the place is neither as wonderful nor as dreadful as portrayed, the inhabitants are both worse and better than anticipated. A period of 'seasoning' follows in each narrative, and the accounts end sometimes in the accepted fashion (marriage and resolution in Long's novel), but more often, resist closure. Many end in a sense of failure, with a further dislocation and relocation. Most haunting, perhaps, is the surprisingly powerful symbolism in Carmichael's generally unimaginative account, of her last West Indian residence prophetically being overrun by large, black 'chasseur ants' who evict the white family and devour all vermin and parasites in their path (Vol 2: 328–333). One is reminded of the white *ajoupa* in *Wide Sargasso Sea*: a vulnerable edifice threatened by the encroaching forest and hordes of woodants that will reduce it to an empty shell. Caroline Rooney's observation (105) is appropriate in this context. The 'colonising enterprise', she maintains, is revealed as 'not just an expression of heartless greed, but an expression of an emptiness or loss of heart at the heart, the supposed source or centre, motivating quests for rejuvenation and reassurance elsewhere'.

I am suggesting, then, that we pay attention to the way in which these narratives by women depart from the conventional tropes of the travel story and the semantic and stylistic implications of such departures. Certainly, recent writers like Jamaica Kincaid and Joan Riley have reversed the 'voyage of discovery' to striking effect, and such re-writings are likely to continue in accounts of the migration experience by West Indian women. Without necessarily claiming the early writers as 'literary foremothers', I would argue that in their *texts*, certain features occur which we see, in different contexts, in later female-authored West Indian fiction.

The outsider's voice

A more tangible connection exists between the twentieth century 'outsider's version' (that of white West Indian writers like Jean Rhys, Phyllis Shand Allfrey and Eliot Bliss) and contemporary fiction by West Indian women. Marginal, yes, as Esteves and Paravisini-Gebert have pointed out, to the nationalist and Afro-centred concerns of the nascent Caribbean literary tradition, they none the less merit a hearing. More poignantly than Mary Seacole's narrative, these women give voice to the agony of the creole's double alienation from 'native' black and European white experience, and detail in a unique way the ambivalence of those just sufficiently colonized to call both England and the Caribbean 'home'.

Additionally, Rhys's *Wide Sargasso Sea*, Bliss's *Luminous Isle* and Allfrey's *The Orchid House* are 'creole' texts in the sense that they are crucially concerned with 'interacting' racial/cultural orientations: with the interpenetration of what Brathwaite has called the 'great' and 'little' traditions. Most students of West Indian literature will be familiar with Rhys's Dominican classic[6] which deals with the attempt and failure of dialogue and interculturation: between local and expatriate whites; between white, black and 'coloured' West Indians; between male and female; between colony and metropolis. The text's structuring principle is articulated by Antoinette: 'there is always the other side. Always.' The reiteration of the mirror symbol, the presentation of Tia as Antoinette's eternal Other, and Antoinette and her husband's mutual disbelief in the reality of each other's worlds (67) are but three examples of the failure to communicate across racial, cultural, psychological and gender divides. The point is that the effort *is* made and the reasons for failure clearly illustrated.

Luminous Isle by Eliot Bliss (born Jamaica, 1903) will be less familiar. The novel chronicles Emmeline Hibbert's childhood in white colonial Jamaican society in the early twentieth century. After an English education, Em returns, a young woman, to rejoin her parents and to play 'her part as their daughter in the social rounds of garrison life in a Crown Colony' (xiii) during the 1920s. But despite her love for the island and her 'affinity' with the black population, Em finds she cannot become integrated into this life of 'perfect Englishness under the hot tropical sun'. As an artist, seeking to lead a free life of the mind without the petty restrictions of class or 'sex-consciousness', she eventually discovers that 'to be sexless, creedless, classless, free' (371) she must leave her beloved Jamaica for a future in the less limiting society of England.

The book anatomizes the life of a privileged child born into the white ruling class of a black country. From the first pages of the text, with the distinction between the 'large white houses' and the 'nigger huts' of the two groups, the interrelationship of and conflicts between classes and nationalities (expatriate and creole white), form the ever-present backdrop to the heroine's development, which in itself leads to the ultimate choice between island colony and metropolis.

Phyllis Shand Allfrey (born Dominica, 1915) sets *The Orchid House* on an island (based on post-colonial Dominica) now ruled by coloured merchants, civil servants and the Catholic church. The novel harks back to a 1920s childhood, but the concern with transitional politics suggests that the bulk of the action takes place in the 1940s – 1950s. Allfrey's theme is a society in flux, mirrored in the microcosm of one white creole family. The old dispensation of the benevolent colonial patriarchy – like Rhys, Allfrey's West Indian roots go back centuries – has given way to that of 'the master', emotionally crippled by his war experiences; in turn, he passes control to the three daughters, Stella, Joan and Natalie, on whom the narrative focuses. Their maturation, departures from and returns to the island, are related by their old black nurse, Lally, and the constant juxtaposition of past and present social orders adds depth to the superficially simple family chronicle.

The text extends the span of political history covered in the other fictions – from Emancipation through Crown Colony to early representative government. Again, the complex interculturation of, and changing relations between, white creole elite, coloured middle class and black peasantry inform the narrative.

As in the other two novels, implicit questions are raised regarding the place and contribution of the white creole minority in the organization of West Indian society: again, the ambivalent relationship of colony/metropole emerges in the white creole's perspective; and the strength of women to survive their sickening men is highlighted. As Lally puts it (164) '[w]omen are always stronger, even up to the death'.

The most striking resemblance between the three texts, however, is their evocation – through their white creole female protagonists – of an ultimately alienated 'outsider' who looks on, but is rarely able to participate in the unfolding drama of West Indian society. Ramchand, as noted previously, claims that such 'elements of continuity' arise primarily from 'the natural stance of the white West Indian' (1972: 224). But Elaine Campbell (1978) suggests that Rhys and Allfrey were aware of each other's writings; and Rhys's letters indicate that she had met Bliss. Whether based on race, culture or familiarity with each other's work one perceives certain similarities in the situations of the alienated fictional women.

All the main female characters belong to families who occupy anomalous and insecure positions in the economic and class hierarchies of their societies. Antoinette's background may be wealthy planter class of English descent, but her mother is 'foreign', a Martiniquan creole, and the family has been reduced to virtual poverty after the post-Emancipation financial crash: they are, as Tia puts it, 'white nigger now, and black nigger better than white nigger' (21). In Bliss's novel, Em is aware (81) that despite their pretensions, the genteel poverty of her family sets them apart:

> It was humiliating to be poor. Rich people with their scornful pitying eyes, or their hypocritical pretence at being 'hard up'; and all the time inside despising one. . . . And the poor despised one as much as the rich for not being able to live up to the standards of the class of people one had been born into.

The white family of *The Orchid House* live in reduced circumstances in the country, supported by their daughters. In addition, the young women of L'Aromatique (like Allfrey and Rhys) are English-speaking Anglicans in a predominantly French Creole-speaking, Catholic population, thus further marginalized.

Secondly, all three novels describe periods of social change: the old order is disappearing, and power is passing from the hands of the white creole elite. It may be relevant to note that Bliss's text was written in the 1930s, a time of growing political unrest in the West Indies; and that *The Orchid House* was published in the 1950s, when most of the islands were demanding independence from British colonial rule. By the time Rhys finished her novel, Dominica as she knew it had changed beyond recognition.

Economic supremacy in these narratives is gradually assumed by the 'new moneyed' entrepreneurs (like the speculator, Mr Mason, in *Wide Sargasso Sea*). As Joan points out in *The Orchid House* (184), the coloured merchants (like Marse Rufus) 'are taking the responsibility over from us – we are now the poor whites, we have no longer any power'. There is no indication in either text that the new order substantially improves the lot of the black peasantry. In *Luminous Isle*, social change is only hinted at ('strange new movements and forces in the world, undercurrents' (92)), but class barriers are relaxing and a young woman has more freedom: Em socializes with people 'whom the parents neither knew nor wholly approved of' (97). Again, wealth changes hands – Americans are buying up more and more of the island (179) – and the novel evokes a pervasive sense of a fading colonial order.

Most importantly, the creole women in these texts inhabit a kind of vacuum regarding their racial/cultural identity. Supposedly 'above' their non-white compatriots (and thus made to deny their coloured relatives), Antoinette and the girls in *The Orchid House* are sneered at by expatriate English whites. Antoinette and Stella are considered suspiciously alien by their metropolitan husbands, and Em in *Luminous Isle* (71) is reminded of the difference between the English and those creoles 'who have lived here for generations'.

In Bliss's novel, planter society is mocked (208) in a way reminiscent of Nugent, and we are told that creole girls 'could not compete [in the husband market] with the fresh young English girls wintering in the Island during the cooler months with a trunkful of new clothes' (128). In these texts, the relationship of England with 'her' colonies rarely transcends the original economic link: as Antoinette says of the British, '[g]old is the idol they worship' (154) and this holds true for her husband's motives in marrying her. Hence, Wally Look Lai's comment on Rhys's text (20) holds good for the others, in that they all touch on 'the theme of the existential chasm that exists between the white West Indian and his [her] ancestors, and the tragic fate which awaits any attempt to bridge this chasm.'

On the other hand, these texts attest to the early narratives' description of the assimilation of 'black' culture in the socialization of white creole children. Hence, the female protagonists all identify to some extent with the black population of the West Indies. Stella's relationship with Lally in *The Orchid House*, echoes that of Antoinette and Christophine in *Wide Sar-*

gasso Sea. Joan, in the former novel, chooses to ally herself with the blacks in their labour and political reform struggles, seeing class rather than race as the root of internal division in the island. In *Luminous Isle*, Em expresses a romanticized view of black people – a criticism also levelled at Michelle Cliff's *Abeng* – when, for example, the narrative enters her consciousness: 'niggers; they fascinated her. There was something restful about black people, and nothing in the least indecent' (4). The last word is crucial: for her, sexual and bodily functions are fine in black women, while repulsive in white women. Obviously, the racial underpinnings of the 'cult of true womanhood' are still very much in place as she writes.

Of course, Em never gets beyond a master-servant relationship with any black person; Antoinette is rejected by her alter-ego, Tia; the jeers that greet Joan's political association with the black Baptiste (who walks three paces behind her, despite his efforts 'not to be too humble' (143)) suggest authorial awareness of the gap that lies between white creole and black. Indeed, one could speculate that the attraction of blacks for the white creole women in the novels is largely an attraction to the opposite *stereotype*, one of a freer, more sensual vitality. Rhys's comment on black people in her autobiography (1979: 50–1) can be construed in this light: 'I decided that they had a better time than we did, they . . . were more alive, more a part of the place than we were', although what is more striking is the aching desire to be of the place, to be 'placed' in the island culture. Em's favourable construction of blacks in *Luminous Isle* is strictly in terms of opposition to 'artificial' white society: blacks are 'naturally rhythmical' (132) in comparison with whites; they are at home with their bodies, while '[i]t is the white people's morality that has made their bodies impure – the sense of *shameful* passion . . . We have lost the power of harmonious joy through our bodies' (251). This is, of course, a textbook example of the kind of ideologically 'contaminated' discourse that Carby describes in her study.

What such racist projections do signify in *Luminous Isle*, is that Em feels herself alienated from the union with her beloved island that black people freely enjoy, alienated by the soul-destroying rigidities of white society to which she belongs, even as she rejects it. In *themselves*, blacks are no more to her than 'aesthetic objects' or servants; in the abstract, they represent an independence from social restrictions and a rootedness in the landscape which she feels she will never achieve.

Christophine's description of Antoinette to the husband in *Wide Sargasso Sea* (128) – 'she is not *béké* like you, but she is *béké*, and not like us either' – applies to all the white creole women in these novels. They are, as Tiffin (1978: 328) puts it, double outsiders, 'condemned to self-consciousness, homelessness, a sense of inescapable difference and even deformity in the two societies by whose judgments' they must always condemn themselves.

The theme of 'homelessness' resurfaces in the depiction of the creole woman's internal tug-of-war between love of native place and the attraction of the good colonial to the Mother Country. An intimate awareness of and immersion in the beauty of the West Indian landscape recurs in the narratives of white creole women: from Symonett's rhapsody on Blue Mountain Peak as 'this elysium on earth' (34) to Bliss's evocation of 'the green-and-gold background of the West Indian home' that draws her protagonist 'back to the Island' (54). A reflection of the alienated consciousness of such characters is their positing of this landscape as the only constant: 'more real than the people sitting on either side of her' (*Luminous Isle,* 100); 'Better, better than people' (*Wide Sargasso Sea,* 24).

However, the metropole also exerts a magnetic pull: for Em, England is the 'real world, the world of chronicle and analysis' (177). Joan, of *The Orchid House,* like Ella in Brodber's *Myal,* is fascinated as a child by fictions 'about life in England. . . .' with its snow that would taste like ice-cream (32). But, with Antoinette, she fails to find any emotional purchase in the 'cardboard world' of the metropole when she encounters it; the grey English landscape proves a disappointing reality for the exiled West Indian of any race.

Finally, gender marginalization contributes to the alienation of the white creole 'outsider' in the texts under review, further consolidating her sense of powerlessness and dislocation. Antoinette, married off to a stranger in *Wide Sargasso Sea,* loses any chance of financial independence and becomes her husband's chattel. In *The Orchid House,* Joan can only pursue her political goals vicariously through her husband and Stella is bound to a man who holds that 'women are designed to be happy around the house, to have children, to be taken care of, to work hard and to take orders!' (105). As for Em in *Luminous Isle,* it is largely the restrictive patriarchal values of colonial life that she flees before she 'learn[s] to become more unreal to herself as she became more like what the world thought a young girl ought to be' (59). In comparison, white male characters (in novels like Ian McDonald's *The Humming Bird Tree* (1969) and Geoffrey Drayton's *Christopher* (1959)) have a far greater sense of security about their place in the hierarchy, their power over their environment (and other races); for them as males, an *active* role is written within colonial discourse. In these male-authored texts, white women are represented as housebound and delicate, peripheral to the core of their children's lives; the vital presences are black servants and nannies. White creole women, then, emerge in the fictions as even further from self-confident agency in their worlds than their male counterparts, given their subsidiary status within an already precarious social group.

West Indian literature has been perenially concerned with 'identity' quests; the white creole woman, as depicted in these three texts, problematizes this issue. With neither blackness, nor 'Englishness', nor economic independence to sustain her, she is excluded from all groups that matter to her and subjected to cruel paradoxes: having privilege without power; sharing oppression without the solidarity and support of fellow victims.[7] The situation of other non-Western fictional characters – like those of Bessie Head, for example – invites comparison. In a sense, the white creole woman suggests a failure of creolization; the product of two cultures, she is denied and despised by both.

Yet the narratives dealt with in this chapter, these *products* of the 'outsider's voice', hardly constitute a failure. Indeed, they bring to West Indian literature an obsessive attention to complexities, and a suspicion of fixed categorization. As D'Costa (1986) notes of Rhys, her 'insider-outsider's treatment of England . . . and the Caribbean gnaws at comfortable ethnocentrisms.' Their unique perspective tends to focus on dissonances, false appearances, 'fissures' in discourse, probing beyond 'the superimposed and made-up personalities that . . . [people] wore, and that one wore sometimes unwillingly oneself (*Luminous Isle*, 56). I would argue that it is precisely because of this ambivalence – their position within West Indian socio-history as apart from, yet inextricably bound up with, the 'broadly ex-African base' – that the 'outsider's voice' needs to be placed within the history of West Indian women's writing.

Further, I think it is possible to situate writers like Rhys and Allfrey (and possibly others) within a local tradition of female intertextuality. In that they foreground, through their fictions, the gaps, the chasms between the cultures they negotiate, such texts are the forerunners of later 'woman versions' which also take up (more obviously oppositional) positions in the deconstruction of colonial myths – texts which I discuss in Chapter 3. Laura Abruna's (1991) discussion of Rhys as a 'literary foremother' for Kincaid's fiction is a good example of this intertextual relationship; and Allfrey's depiction of a white creole woman who deliberately situates herself within the struggle for black political liberation seems to me to prefigure Clare Savage's casting her lot with black revolutionaries in Michelle Cliff's *No Telephone to Heaven*. Cliff's text also treats of the problematic pull between Mother Country and island home (the country interestingly, of the *grandmother*) for the white woman, a theme that surfaces in West Indian literature by women (and men) up to the present day; Caryl Phillips's *Cambridge* is a case in point.

I do not want, in any sense, to downplay the importance of race and class differences in West Indian women's writing; but my premise – that any theoretical formulation about this literature be inclusive, making a space for *all* voices (however problematic in terms of historical/racial/political context) whether or not they fit into pre-set agendas in the construction of a 'politically correct' West Indian canon – precludes the kind of dismissal of the 'outsider's voice' with which I began this chapter. We can, perhaps, benefit from Henry Louis Gates Jr's comment on black American woman writers (1990: 8):

> they have learned from some of the early missteps of both the black nationalist and women's movements. In any event, having been excluded from representational authority for so long, black feminists have declined to respond with a counter-politics of exclusion. They have never been obsessed with arriving at any singular self-image; or legislating who may or may not speak on the subject; or policing boundaries between 'us' and 'them'.

Such 'an embracive politics of inclusion' seems to me an admirable strategy to adopt in theorizing about West Indian fiction by women.

Notes

1   The Senate House Library, University of London, for example, contains the correspondence of Jane Lane (MS 523/690) with her master in 1813, requesting the freedom of her two sons. E.B. Underhill, in *The West Indies* (New York: Negro Universities Press, 1970: 21–23) relates the story of Maria Jones who, after emancipation, learned to read at sixty years of age.

2   The anonymous verse, 'Me Know No Law, Me Know No Sin', appears in J.B. Moreton's *West India Customs and Manners* (London: J. Parsons, 1973 (Second Edition): 153).

3   Indeed, Brathwaite (1970: 6) has expressed reservations about the 'frightening gap' between educated, middle-class (and, presumably, non-white) writers of 'peasant' or 'yard' fiction, and the actual underprivileged folk they ˙epresent in such texts. This suggestion is that there is also a lack in such writers' 'recognition of the realities of the situation.'

4   See, for example, Fenwick (163, 168, 171, 175); Carmichael (Vol 1: 22–3, 263).

5   See Beckles's citation (69) of Pinckard's account of this phenomenon, witnessed in Barbados at the end of the 1790s, and the embarrassment of *foreign* guests at the sight of a white child drawing sustenance from the black breast, while the *creole* ladies treated the scene with great familiarity.

6   Despite the Jamaican setting, Rhys has drawn on Dominican history and geography in the portrayal of place. For example, her mother's family, the Lockharts, owned a rural plantation called 'Geneva' (clearly the model for Coulibri) which was burned to the ground in 1932 as a 'political gesture'.

7   Nunez-Harrell (281) claims that 'the peasant class in the West Indies is quick to understand that the white creole woman shares its status of the underclass and underprivileged'. In the novels discussed here, there's no evidence of any sympathetic inclusion of the white women in the 'underclass' category by black characters.

CHAPTER 2 | 'Madwoman' version

In the previous chapter, I pointed out the necessary link between the historical context of textual production, and the influence of dominant European ideologies of femininity in the writing of West Indian women. Bush's observation (14), that black women in the slavery period tended to be portrayed by *both* planter and abolitionist as a composite of 'scarlet woman', domineering matriarch and passive workhorse, calls attention to the *interpretative* factors underlying such portrayals. Contemporary European ideo-logy held that decent/white women were modest in their dress; thus the 'impudent nakedness' of African women was construed as evidence of lewdness.

Of course, as noted earlier, ideology can reinforce the maintenance of power relations. So, as Bush (12) explains, after the end of white indentureship in the West Indies it was necessary to minimize distinctions between classes of white women by maximizing distinctions between black and white women, thus 'establishing the social position' of *all* whites; and the stereotyping of women according to race (ideal, chaste – white; inferior, immoral – black) enabled the ideological justification of hierarchical relations. Throughout the slavery and colonial periods of West Indian history, then, certain stereotypes of women – circulated in the media, in fiction and 'edifying' works – related less to the material reality of women's lives than to discursive maintenance of a specific hierarchy of power.

Brodber's (1982) study of images of black women in Barbados, Jamaica and Trinidad from the post-Emancipation period to independence, details the strategies by which stereotypes are crystallized, disseminated and adopted – even by the very women stereotyped. She points up the disparity between the actual lives of working-class black women and the 'ideal' images of women portrayed via the media, images like 'Excellent Ellen' and 'Household Pearl', the fair-skinned, cultivated, middle-class wife and mother, the decorative yet resourceful 'Angel of the House' (15–16; 22–24). Certainly, the difference was apparent to the assertive, self-confident and often financially independent black women Brodber describes in the early twentieth century West Indies. But one must take Merle Hodge's point, in her introduction to Brodber's text (viii–xiii), that the promotion of 'ideal' stereotypes can negatively impact on how 'real' women perceive and evaluate themselves.

Cobham (1990) corroborates Brodber's findings: the actual lives of most Jamaican women, their familial and sexual alliances, were quite different from the 'ideal' images of femininity promoted in the media and male-authored texts in the first part of the century. But even where working-class women were admired for their industry, they were censured for falling short of the moral high ground of the 'Angel of the House', who was bound by economic dependency to sexual fidelity to a single male. As Cobham demonstrates, the actual stereotyping of women might change – working-class militancy in Jamaica led to idealization of black women mid-century, via stereotypes such as 'enduring mother of the race' or beautiful African princess – but they remain within the norms of patri-archal discourse, whether colonial or nationalist. And stereotypes can be damaging for the self-assessment of women who judge themselves according to the 'ideal'.

A consistently popular, if currently unfashionable, approach to female-authored work has been the study of fictional 'images of women' as reflecting or subverting current notions of femininity. This holds true for West Indian women's writing; indeed, it was a consistently popular focus for my students' essays. In this chapter I want to attend to a specific image that recurs in the fiction – that of the 'madwoman', an alienated and psychologically fragmented figure – and to isolate some of the female stereotypes which are partially the *cause* of her condition.

The voice of the madwoman – the ultimate outsider – has been remarked on by Mordecai and Wilson (xii) who speculate whether a certain surrealist quality may not emerge 'from an early and persistent preoccupation with madness – "*la folie antillaise*" – on the part of Caribbean women writers . . . .' Certainly, Marie-Denise Shelton (350–52) notes similarities (despite race and class circumstances) in the depiction of female protagonists by francophone women authors, protagonists who withdraw into worlds of fantasy, or seek refuge in suicide or symbolic self-annihilation. Shelton observes that this condition is a result of the characters' inability to find a place in their societies, their feelings of abnormality, an 'existential disease of belonging nowhere, of being deprived of identity' (351). Accordingly, she considers this fictional focus as highlighting 'the contradictions and tensions characteristic of feminine existence in the Caribbean' (352); and it is such 'contradictions and tensions' within Caribbean female experience that I want to explore in Miriam Warner-Viera's *As the Sorcerer Said*, Zee Edgell's *Beka Lamb* and Rhys's *Wide Sargasso Sea*. Warner-Viera's novel was originally published in French (Paris: Présenca Africaine, 1980) and properly belongs to the francophone Caribbean. However, in the light of Shelton's remarks, I want to make an exception here to my anglophane focus in order to explore a regionally inscribed phenomenon in women's fiction.

The image of the madwoman occurs in other texts also: in Brodber's *Myal* for example, and it is central to her earlier novel *Jane and Louisa Will Soon Come Home*, in which the female protagonist suffers a physical and mental breakdown, a fragmentation of self out of which she is beginning to emerge whole as the novel ends. A similar process is undergone by the very different central character in Paule Marshall's *Praisesong for the Widow*, while Elizabeth in Marion Patrick-Jones's *Jou'vert Morning* becomes a crazy woman walking the streets. The young protagonists of Kincaid's *Annie John*, Hodge's *Crick Crack Monkey* and Joan Riley's *The Unbelonging* all evince various stages of excessive withdrawal and physical and emotional collapse.

In the three texts I've chosen to focus on, the female characters manifest a form of psychosis in their near-total flight from 'reality' and end up incarcerated or institutionalized. Interestingly, this does not reflect trends in the distribution of mental disorders among West Indian women.[1] Despite differences of historical context, social origin and race, Warner-Viera's Suzette (Zetou), Edgell's Toycie and Rhys's Antoinette display similar personality traits. They are described in adolescence as insecure, vulnerable and – as in several of the other novels mentioned – share a history of parental loss, rejection or enforced separation. Growing up, they experience loneliness and powerlessness, exacerbated in the cases of Zetou and Antoinette (like Riley's Hyacinth, and Brodber's Ella in *Myal*) by physical displacement. Further rejection or betrayal follows: Zetou is raped by her mother's lover; Toycie is deserted by the boyfriend who has made her pregnant, and expelled from her school; Antoinette is betrayed, humiliated and finally locked up by her husband. All react, understandably, with anger, guilt, fear, frustration and hopelessness. They exhibit behavioural 'abnormalities' such as extreme violence, paranoia and hallucination, finally being judged insane. Toycie and Antoinette demonstrate self-destructive tendencies, and Zetou implicitly wishes for death as a release.

While heeding Lillian Feder's warning (10) that 'attempts at diagnoses of the pathology of fictive characters by literary critics are often anachronistic, not to say absurd,' it is hard not to see in these fictional 'case studies' almost classic symptoms of schizophrenia.[2] Again, Shelton's comments (352) are useful. In the francophone texts she refers to, the female protagonists experience 'an internal police state' which impedes all normal life activities; some feel the world to be threatening and are 'drawn into a solipsistic existence in which there is no other reality but the self, yet withdrawal into the self does not produce a sense of security' (352) but ultimately, disintegration. Her observations seem to me to bear a striking resemblance to R.D. Laing's depiction of schizophrenia in *The Divided Self*, the central concepts of which are worth briefly synopsizing here. After all, discordance is an important element in the dub version!

Laing – writing at a period when the notion of an integrated 'self' had not yet been destabilized, as has subsequently become the case – holds that most people experience themselves as conscious subjects, mind and body integrated, interacting with a world which is made up of other objects, including other persons (who, by analogy, are also presumed to be autonomous, integrated subjects). But there are exceptions, such as the 'schizoid' person:

> Such a person is not able to experience himself 'together with' others or 'at home in' the world but, on the contrary, he experiences himself in despairing aloneness and isolation; moreover, he does not experience himself as a complete person but rather as 'split' in various ways, perhaps as a mind more or less tenuously linked to a body, as two or more selves, and so on. (15)

This person suffers from 'ontological insecurity'; he or she lacks the sense of unquestioning, self-validating, integral selfhood and personal identity that 'normal' people take for granted – and that what we call 'postmodernism' has, with same controversy, called into question. Thus he or she seeks isolation, and avoids relationships with other subjects, who may 'absorb' him or her as just another thing in the world of objects; complete isolation is a defence against the threat of complete merging of identity with another.

The ontologically insecure person doesn't even feel an integration of self (mind) and body – the latter is perceived as a detached thing, another object in the world of depersonalized objects. The unembodied 'true self' looks on detachedly as the body (the 'false self' or 'false self system') plays its part/parts. We've all felt such dissociation ('this is like a dream'; 'this isn't happening to me'), but for 'normal' people the feeling of disembodiment is temporary. This 'false self' of the schizoid usually acts according to other people's standards and expectations, having none of its own, thus concealing and protecting the true self. As Laing points out, such compliance with 'what other people say I am' is a betrayal of one's true potential, a concept imaginatively conveyed in the 'kumbla' image in Erna Brodber's first novel.[3] In the West Indian Context, one could argue that the type of 'abnormality' termed schizophrenia here is presented in the literature as a natural extension of the kumbla survival strategy, and therefore complicates simplistic notions of 'identity' implied in my straightforward mapping of Laing's theory onto the writing. However, in the interests of pursuing his model, I would wish to bracket such questions for now; the issue of the 'unified subject' informs Chapter 4.

Behind the facade of the false self/selves, the isolated 'true self' becomes more and more empty, a vacuum, having no direct connection with the world, omnipotent in fantasy, but powerless to control events in actuality. In time, this 'true self' becomes increasingly critical of the false self, now considered to be separate, to belong to the hostile world of others. One thinks of Kincaid's eponymous Lucy admitting that 'I was then at the height of my two-facedness: that is, outside I seemed one way, inside I was another; outside false, inside true' (18). The 'false self' behaves like the nice young lady her mother has taught her to be; the 'true self' rages at this hypocrisy. In the final stages of dissociation, the schizoid become schizophrenic, becomes psychotic: he or she feels unreal, 'dead' and wishes for death, that of the imprisoning torture-chamber which the 'true-self' (the mind) has become.

Laing's description of the ontologically insecure consciousness is echoed in the fictions discussed here; a comparison of passages from *As the Sorcerer Said* (72–3) and *The Divided Self* (164, 166) reveals noticeable similarities in depiction of feeling, response and use of imagery. Toycie, in *Beka Lamb* (134), studying her imaginary schoolwork intently, is reminiscent of Laing's portrait of the schizophrenic trying to 'acquire' reality, from which the 'true self' is isolated, by copying or imitating forms of behaviour perceived as real. And in Rhys's text, there are numerous instances when the vivid portrayal of Antoinette's disturbance conforms to symptoms described by Laing: for example, her perception of the world as meaningless, colourless, unreal (148); the split between her 'real' self and the ghostly self she sees in the mirror (147); the importance of touching her red dress as a link with reality (152); and her self-conception as two entities, a 'she' and an 'I' (154).

As Elizabeth Abel (157) points out, Laing's attempts to reconstruct the schizophrenic's way of being in the world (rather than attempting to describe it objectively), has certain parallels with literary exegisis. And so she makes a bold step from psychoanalytic to literary theory, examining several Rhysian novels in the light of Laing's paradigm of the divided self. Her treatment of *Wide Sargasso Sea* focuses on reader response to the conflicting narratives of the 'mad' Antoinette (whose point of view is intensely subjective and emotive) and the 'sane' husband (who maintains a facade of intellectual objectivity about events). Abel suggests Rhys's text implies that we grant excessive authority to the latter perspective. However, it can be argued that several manifestations of the husband's behaviour *also* bear close resemblance to Laing's schizoid characteristics: for example, his crazed possessiveness; his deliberate depersonalization of Antoinette; his fear of being engulfed by the tropical landscape/the passion of his wife; his insistence on protecting, hiding his inner self. Indeed, Laing's study of the patient 'James', who reifies his wife into an 'it' with a 'robot-like nature'

(50–51), because of his own ontological insecurity, suggests that the husband's sane, sensible world view in *Wide Sargasso Sea* is actually flawed and precarious. Indeed, I would query – as does Paula Anderson (1981) – whether we *do* 'know objectively that Antoinette is mad', as Abel claims (175).

But to return to the negative power of stereotypes. Abel's attempt to discover reasons for the helpless, divided state of Rhys's heroines utilizes Laing's suggestion that ontological insecurity is due in part to parental failure in instilling a sense of autonomy in the child, instead valuing passive compliance and submissiveness as model behaviour. Such failure, she explains *pace* Laing, 'leads the child to question (or never to develop) an independent sense of self, to feel susceptible to the control of external forces' (168).

Obviously, this is particularly the case in the socialization of girl-children into an ideal notion of femininity which, as Brodber explains (1982: 32), was summed up in the stereotype of woman (the fair-skinned, middle-class Eurocentric woman, in the West Indian media) as 'delicate, diffident, tender, pleasing, tactful, suffering and at home'. Good behaviour for girls, by such standards – the standards of those wishing upward mobility for their charges – meant being compliant, obedient, self-effacing and submissive. Toycie, in *Beka Lamb*, is a model child, a model student, a model young lady, her anxiety to please and conform reinforced by her precarious economic situation as a woman in her society (34) and her desire to become 'somebody'. Abel makes the link (169) between submissive femininity and ontological insecurity, positing 'a continuum between the general lack of confidence produced in women by cultural attitudes and the radical lack of self characteristic of schizophrenia.' Gilbert and Gubar (54) are quite specific about the negative effects of patriarchal socialization on women's mental, and physical, health: 'To be trained in renunciation is almost necessarily to be trained in ill health, since the human animal's first and strongest urge is to his or her *own* survival, pleasure, assertion. . . .' What I want to suggest, then, is that it is possible to make connections between the ideal image of the 'Angel in the House', repression of will in women, and self-doubt and psychic dysfunction in several texts by West Indian women writers.

Of course, the specifics of the region's history of colonialism have also to be taken into account. The colonized, taught to value him or herself according to the standards of empire, necessarily experienced impotence, powerlessness and insecurity: and severe alienation as well as the condition of self-division, is a recurrent theme in West Indian literature as a whole. In this context, Antoinette, Tee and Zetou (along with Ella in *Myal*) look to the world of books, snow and 'The Miller's Daughter', and find their own worlds lacking in comparison, their own lives unreal by such standards. However, I want to focus at present on the way 'colonial' factors, with their race/class underpinnings, are complicated by the issue of gender in these texts.

The characters in all three novels grow up in changing societies where social mobility for women is accessible via several channels, all of which involve conflict in terms of social/sexual roles. Like Toycie, Zetou conceives of a different future for herself than that of the women in her village since 'the idea of having nothing but housework and children to occupy my time later was most depressing' (28–9). Education is a way out of poverty and limited options. But Zetou's family considers educating a *female*, especially one of her class, to be useless and even dangerous, while in *Beka Lamb* the author relates that 'economic necessity forced many creole girls to leave school after elementary education' (34). As the testimonies of Sistren's *Lionheart Gal* reiterate, the fact of gender determines the priority for limited educational opportunities. Consider the narrator of 'Country Madda Legacy': 'Me was finishing Senior School and me did waan go a High School. Me tell him [her father]. Him say, 'Cho! Me nah spend no money pon gal pickney, because dem a go look man'' (70).

Further, social mobility via education entails internalization of ideal stereotypes of womanhood, passed on by foreign-trained school authorities. So in *Beka Lamb*, the convent school offers an alternative future for girls to 'the washing bowl underneath the house bottom' (2), but to graduate they must 'leap through the hoops of quality purposely held high by the nuns' (112). And for many, these 'hoops of quality' represent norms that clash with those of their indigenous working-class society (which they are expected to deny once inside the convent gates).

One clash involves conceptions of female sexuality. As noted in Chapter 1, this implied very different models of behaviour, dependent on a woman's race, during the plantation era. A similar duality operates in the case of Toycie, whose working-class background countenances unmarried motherhood and a degree of sexual freedom for women, but whose rise up the social ladder (via schooling) involves emulation of the Virgin Mary. Her illegitimate pregnancy thus brands her, in the eyes of the school authorities, as yet another black woman who can't say no. 'We women must learn to control our emotions' preaches Sister Virgil (120), and Toycie's expulsion is a harsh lesson to Beka Lamb on the constraints placed on female sexuality in Sister Virgil's world. Choice of social role is thus inevitably bound up with a binary choice between virgin/whore stereotypes, as made clear by Father Nunez (90) in his lectures to the schoolgirls. A similar, if more complex choice, faces Miss Coolie in Olive Senior's story, 'Arrival of the Snake Woman'; to be socially acceptable, and thus to have access to education and material advancement is to renounce 'heathen' ways in which woman is constructed in terms of sexual temptress. When the pregnant Toycie vomits on the chapel floor, she is established in the eyes of authority (religious and educational) as a source of contamination, to be removed before her sin, like Eve's, infects other girls.

For Antoinette, social respectability is linked to marriage, but here too sexuality is problematic. Her English husband considers her alien, tainted – by the standards of the 'cult of ideal womanhood' – largely because her sexual abandon, into which he has initiated her, signals her intrinsically promiscuous, not to say unbalanced nature:

> She thirsts for *anyone* – not for me . . . (a mad girl. She'll not care who she's loving). She'll moan and cry and give herself as no sane woman would – or could. *Or could.* (135–6).

Zetou has also been socialized into the image of the female as a standard of chastity and her rape by her mother's lover devastates her, incurring feelings of guilt and degradation: 'I was sharing a man with my mother, I was damning my own soul' (66). For all three characters, models of female sexuality involve an 'either/or' choice, the making of which results in confusion, guilt and eventually, madness.

Where social status cannot be achieved through formal schooling or marriage, it is often associated for women with dependency on a man. Zetou's light-skinned mother escapes poverty and reaches Paris as the mistress of a Frenchman who demands she 'give herself airs of a fine lady' (57) to hide her humble origins. Antoinette's mother, widowed, impoverished and socially 'marooned' sees 'catching' a man as the only hope for her family. Indeed, the novels are short on positive role-models of independent womanhood. In *Beka Lamb*, Miss Eila (Toycie's guardian) depreciates herself as ugly and thus unmarriageable, and even Beka's strong Granny Ivy is denied the vote and must live according to her son's rule. The women in Zetou's village raise children and serve men; her self-sufficient grandmother upholds the view that a woman's life consists of cooking, mending and housekeeping (22). And in *Wide Sargasso Sea*, the older women are virtually all victims: Antoinette's mother is a crazed lunatic; Aunt Cora, ageing and powerless, turns her face to the wall; even the redoubtable Christophine admits that she has been a fool in her dealings with men (91) and ultimately yields the narrative to Antoinette's husband.

To be a 'respectable' woman in these texts involves economic dependence on a man – father-figure, lover, husband – which confers the status of chattel: Antoinette, once 'sold' by her stepfather to a husband, has no legal rights to her inheritance; Zetou's mother colludes with her lover to marry her daughter off to a rich white man for a price. The 'ideal' woman is also submissive to the superior male, with the devolution of agency this entails. Antoinette gives her husband control over her very existence: 'Say die and I will die,' she tells him (77). To emulate the *opposite* of respectable is to incur the wrath of society and the Church, to become, in effect, no better than the prostitute National Vellour in *Beka Lamb*, a scorned and feared outcast.

Anxiety over choice of social (class-based) and sexual affiliation is compounded in the Caribbean context of these texts by the alienation of the colonial, educated into self-contempt: 'nothing from Cocotier had any value' says Zetou's mother (45), including herself or her daughter. Such anxiety is imaged in several novels as an internal weight or growth, some-times cold and suffocating (Edgell, 25; Kincaid, 85; Brodber, 1980: 24; 1988: 92) and an inversion of the positive image of female conception of new life.

Initially, female characters adopt defence mechanisms. One method of protecting the insecure self from the hostile claims of the world is, as Laing explains, the adoption of one or more roles/'false selves'; that is,

> becoming what the other person wants or expects one to become while only being one's 'self' in imagination. . . . In conformity, therefore, with what one perceives or fancies to be the *thing* one is in the other person's eyes, the false self becomes that thing (105).

Zetou, for example, responds to the gradual erosion of her sense of inte-grated self by objectifying her actions in theatrical terminology (62) until she realizes that the role is *not* temporary, that her 'true self' is totally subsumed in the 'false self': 'I was no longer on a stage, playing my part opposite other actors. The curtain would never fall, never, as I was playing my own role' (65). In Edgell's novel, Beka's role-playing in the face of a threatening reality, her lies about herself and her achievements, threaten to take her over. And, as Laing observes, to 'play one's own role', to become a 'thing' for others leads to the virtual autonomy of the 'false self' over which the true self can exert no control. Fictional representations of such 'false selves' include the 'cracked doll' that Nellie becomes in *Jane and Louisa Will Soon Come Home*; the eternal schoolgirl Toycie plays to her death in *Beka Lamb*; and, in *Crick Crack Monkey*, Tee's self-invented ideal double, Helen, who 'was the proper Me. And Me, I was her shadow, hovering about in incompleteness' (62).

The shadow 'Me' has autonomy only in fantasy or, as Laing puts it, 'in games in front of a mirror' (105).[4] This latter is an important symbol in *Wide Sargasso Sea*, for Antoinette is literally and figuratively obsessed with mirrors as she vainly seeks a viable self-image in the models of womanhood offered her: the English 'Miller's Daughter' (30); her double/ opposite, the black Tia (38); the perfect young da Plana ladies at the convent school (46), and so on. As Antoinette becomes more disturbed, the image of the mirror is used to suggest the widening gap between her real and false selves, or role/s:

The girl I saw [in the glass] was myself yet not quite myself. Long ago when I was a child and very lonely I tried to kiss her. But the glass was between us . . . (147).

The dissociation becomes more severe ('I saw Antoinette drifting out of the window', she thinks (147)), until at the worst stage of her madness, the psychic split is complete and she no longer recognizes herself in the mirror, '*The woman* with streaming hair. *She* was surrounded by a gilt frame but *I* knew her' (154, my emphases).

Laing's paradigm of the true self, isolated from the false self/selves which play out roles to please others, finally 'haunted' and driven mad by those selves that become autonomous, seems similar to the process dramatized in the development of the fictional madwomen analyzed here. The choice of roles (self-images) is determined by the social context of each novel, but the device of assuming roles is clearly a defensive one. For these characters, reality offers no possibility of integrated self-images – hence Zetou describes herself and her fellow patients as 'people for whom madness was the only solution to a desperate situation' (52). However, the defensive strategy is ultimately counter-productive as dissociation occurs, and even the 'inner self' is fragmented in madness.

This dysfunctional awareness of self as a mirror of external models, and at the expense of one's own autonomy, is echoed in Brodber's findings on the effects of internalizing female stereotypes (1982: 55). As we've seen, many such stereotypes are pernicious for female agency, and the image of the 'ideal' woman whose purpose and being ultimately derive from another has obvious parallels with that of the ideal 'native', written by and taught to conform to imperial discourse. In both cases, psychic fragmentation (born of frustration and trivialization by ideological means) may be articulated in terms of an awareness of victimization, a natural correlative of powerlessness.

And if 'the colonized' is a victim within colonial discourse, the colonized 'madwoman' is triply so. What option but to opt out? Phyllis Chesler (1972) goes so far as suggesting that many women institutionalized in mental hospitals are there in protest against their devalued female role. At the risk of conflating medical and literary 'cases', Toycie, Zetou and Antoinette do appear to have 'given in', to have sought refuge in the pose of isolated victim craving the ultimate withdrawal into death. The final description of Zetou is almost foetal – like Annie John, 'curled up like a little comma' (126) during her period of collapse – paralleling Hyacinth's state at the close of *The Unbelonging*, and suggests the extent of passive acceptance of their fate to which these 'madwomen' have come. Women divided – by cultures, classes, roles, places, gender stereotypes – they are reduced in the end to empty flesh, to 'zombies'.[5]

Barbara Lalla (1992) offers an original linguistic perspective on Antoinette's death-in-life state in *Wide Sargasso Sea*. She argues that Antoinette's multilingualism mirrors, to some extent, her lack of definition. Able to communicate across speech-codes, she is made aware 'that different worlds are confronting each other without understanding, and that she can never fully be a part of any of them' (11). Thus, language is instrumental in maintaining power differentials between groups (14). No wonder Antoinette seeks refuge in silence, telling her husband 'words are no use, I know that now' (*Wide Sargasso Sea*, 111). Communication – between the world as defined by English textuality and the world of orality and folk beliefs, the world of English man and that of creole woman – seems futile, and Antoinette is 'marooned' somewhere in between, trapped in her attic void.

Indeed, Rhys's text is perhaps the best fictional illustration of Laing's concept of ontological insecurity, and – with *Jane and Louisa* – represents the complex demands of gender roles/options, racial stratification and colonial double loyalties that combine to fragment both individuals and societies. Here, one can see West Indian women writers reinterpreting the 'quest for identity' theme pervasive in regional literature, using the 'madwoman' as metonymic of the debilitating 'illness' of the self which still haunts Caribbean societies in the wake of the colonial encounter. Additionally, a more gender-specific reading emphasizes the problematic nature of the very term 'female identity' and the pernicious influence of restrictive and/or polarized stereotyping of West Indian women.

To conclude, I want to return briefly to Laing and his later suggestion – raised by Feder (281) and Abel (173) – of madness as a kind of liberation from constraining attitudes and values, an alternative to 'opting out' that can lead to a rebirth of an integrated self. For Abel, madness (in the specific schizophrenic use of the term) may involve breakthrough as well as breakdown. Hence, she finds in Antoinette's final dream a transcendence of the 'false self' or ghost she has become, and a movement toward recovery of subjectivity and agency. Antoinette's waking words, '[s]omeone screamed and I thought, *Why did I scream*' (155), signify for Abel (174) a reidentification of 'someone' with 'I', suggesting a resolution of the divided state which is emphasized by the narrative choice of *present* tense for Antoinette's final statement of awareness and future intent.

Lalla's insightful comment on this tense shifting highlights the novel's lack of closure, since what has gone before 'remains part of an account in the past of the speaker' (19) and what is to come remains open to interpretation. This, Lalla feels, frees *Wide Sargasso Sea* from intertextual dependency on Bronte's *Jane Eyre*, as far as the 'inevitable' fate of the 'mad' creole is concerned.

In addition, Lalla calls attention to the formal qualities of Rhys's text (shifts in time/space/speaking voice) which unfasten 'the normal anchors' on which readers rely. Daryl Dance's treatment of *Jane and Louisa* (1990: 181–2) as a journey from madness to sanity, similarly focuses on the refusal of linear development in the novel, its fluidity in respect to time/space/ narrative point of view, and its narrative progress through slowly accreted links between words, tones, phrases and moods. Additionally, Dance notes the text's negotiation of 'the worlds of the living, the dead, the actual, and the dream/fantasy/rumour' (182). Perhaps one can read into such comments a textual strategy for evasion of limitation by the restrictive mimetic realm of surface realism, for suggesting through fractured language and form an alternative, *liberating* consciousness of the world.

Similarly, it is possible to view the madwoman's strategy of 'opting out' of *all* role models/images/stereotypes as a refusal, if not a deconstruction, of the arbitrary boundaries of a divided patriarchal colonial society. The characters mentioned react to impossible demands for conformity by refusing to engage with the 'normal' on its terms to opt out, as it were, of the 'subject positions' on offer. While I would not dismiss Feder's caution (286) about the 'present vogue' for associating madness with wisdom, neither do I consider that the recurring figure of the madwoman in West Indian women's fiction reflects the tragic nature of the female condition for many women in the region. Rather, it seems to me that attention to the 'madwoman's voice', with its implicit interrogation of distinctions between normal and sane versus aberrant and mad, illuminates the impossible straitjackets of polarized female stereotypes into which girlchildren in the Caribbean were – and to some extent, still are – required to fit. Obviously, the texts mentioned do not recommend insanity as a means of overcoming stereotyping. Confrontation with contradictory and frustrating 'images of woman' *may* lead (with Nellie in Brodber's novel) towards reconstruction of self; in other cases, engagement with such issues overwhelms and fragments the female character.

Balutansky (forthcoming, 5) argues against any reading that 'reinscribes reductive and stereotypical notions of Caribbean women's "identity" by privileging sociological or racial notions of "authenticity".' It seems to me that the texts discussed in this chapter counter such a reading, not by creating positive 'images of woman' in reaction to debilitating stereotypes popularized in colonial/patriarchal discourse, but by demonstrating through the predicament of the alienated, victimized madwoman the futility of *all* female stereotypes as life-models. Further, the fictions emphasize the *constructed* nature of polarized inscriptions of female sexuality so long employed to manage women, and to buttress the colonial enterprise in the West Indies.

Theoretical reflections on West Indian literature then, can benefit from attending to the discordant 'madwoman version' by taking into account such textual resistance to interpellation according to *any* rigid, 'normative' dictates about what it means to be a woman of or in the region.

Notes

1   Aggrey Burke's data from Trinidad and Tobago ('Socio-cultural determinants of psychiatric disorder among women in Trinidad and Tobago', *West Indian Medical Journal*, 23, (1974) pp. 75–79) lists 'affective disorders' (those associated primarily with acute mood changes, such as depression and hypomania) as the most common illnesses among the female patients in the psychiatric unit. These are 'functional disorders' – that is, there is no demonstrable organic cause, like brain tumour, for the symptoms, so illness is due to environmental stress and/or endogenous factors such as biochemistry and, perhaps, genetic make-up. After the affective disorders, Burke ranks schizophrenia (a psychosis), then neuroses (such as phobias) and finally personality disorders. A small percentage of his sample was categorized 'no diagnosis', which consisted of young women with 'situation or adjustment reactions' and included attempted suicides. Organic disorders and 'other diagnoses' made up the rest of the sample. He notes that most of the patients admitted to the psychiatric unit were in the younger age group (about half were under 25) and both admission rates and diagnosis categories for the East Indian and African subcultural groups were similar.

    There will be notable differences between admissions to a psychiatric unit in a hospital and to a public mental hospital, which tends to be a 'last resort' for the very disturbed or the very poor. Dut Dr Ermine Belle, of the Barbados Mental Hospital, also lists depression and hypomania as the most common mental illnesses among admitted patients. After these come psycho-neuroses, personality disorders and other diagnoses, with psychoses like schizophrenia and manic-depression being much rarer. For further amplification of Dr Belle's comments, see O'Callaghan (1985).

2   Nevertheless, as Rack (99) reminds us, '[c]ultural differences in the manifestations of distress and the way such manifestations are interpreted, represent *diagnostic pitfalls* for the practitioner. . . .' Thus 'classic' symptoms of an illness may be perceived as evidence of quite another condition in the patient's own society.

3   Brodber's symbol of the kumbla, in *Jane and Louisa*, is represented as a protective enclosure, a calabash or cocoon, built out of layers of assumed roles behind which the fragile self shelters. The vulnerability of the self is relevant here. But, as the novel makes clear (130), '[i]f you dwell too long in it, it makes you delicate.' Protective camouflage is a temporary measure; eventually, the self must form by engaging with a threatening world or risk further fragmentation.

4   Lacan's 'mirror stage' suggests itself here. For Lacan, it is in the mirrored image of self (which is also *not* self) that the infant begins to construct a centred notion of self. However, as Eagleton points out (165), this image is 'alienated' in that the reflection suggests a pleasing unity which the child does not experience in its own body. Justifying a sense of an 'I' through finding it reflected back by some object/person – as Antoinette tries to do – is part of the 'imaginary' state and Lacan notes the *fictive* nature of a unitary selfhood thus produced.

5   See Rhys's *Letters* (1985) p. 263. The term will take on further nuances in Chapter 4, where its centrality to Brodber's *Myal* is discussed.

CHAPTER 3

Post-'it' notes: post-colonial feminist readings

Post-colonial theory

The model of the dub version outlined earlier suggests an analogous literary strategy which disturbs the distinction between privileged, original 'substantive' narrative, and marginal, inferior, 'copy' versions. If one sees the author rather like a sound engineer who plays around with the master tape, then the original becomes public property and – as medieval poets did with the common plots and motifs of romance – each artist is free to alter, borrow, cannibalize and adapt constituent elements in the production of a new creation. To an extent, feminist theories have approached women's writing in a similar light: as subversive re-writings of the male canon, which destabilize it in the process. Within the last two decades, post-colonial literary theory has also focused on such strategies in its consideration of literary texts (from territories that share a history of colonialism) as interrogating and dismantling assumptions within imperial discourse.

Like 'feminist theory', post-colonial theory presents problems of definition; it might be well to begin with Slemon and Tiffin's (1989: ix) concept of post-colonial *literature* as 'writing that is grounded in the cultural realities of those societies whose subjectivity has been constituted at least in part by the subordinating power of European colonialism.' Post-colonial theory, then, attends to this 'background' of what H. Adlai Murdoch calls 'marginalization and . . . subjection to a colonial discourse' out of which post-colonial literatures are seen to 'establish a cultural and discursive identity of their own' (2). Power relations between European centre and marginal colony; the methods by which the colonizer appropriates and inscribes the colonized as inferior, as lack, as negation; the structural opposition – JanMohammed's 'Manichean aesthetic' – that makes possible such inscription: these are some aspects of colonial hegemony that post-colonial writing interrogates, resists and subverts. *How* it does so is the subject of post-colonial theory.

Language is one of the most important sites of resistance. Ashcroft, Griffiths and Tiffin (38) theorize that literary decolonization occurs first through *abrogation* – 'a refusal of the categories of the imperial culture, its aesthetic, its illusory standard of normative or "correct" usage, and its assumption of a traditional and fixed meaning "inscribed" in the words' – and then by *appropriation* of the colonizer's language which is made to '"bear the burden" of one's own cultural experience. . . .' Other key concerns in the literature include notions of place and displacement, the importance of hybridity and syncreticity, and formal/stylistic strategies for articulating the silenced colonial subject.

It does seem obvious then, as Davies and Fido point out (2), that 'Caribbean women's writing . . . has to be understood first within the context of the various imperialist discourses and then against them as a rewriting of those discourses.' Therefore post-colonial theory – even in the very simplified version outlined above – will provide useful avenues of approach to West Indian fiction by women. However, the literature has also to be considered in relation to patriarchal discourse in post-colonial societies. I think we have to be very clear on the fact that patriarchal oppression is not an abstract concept for many West Indian women. Carole Boyce Davies, in the forward to *Out of the Kumbla* (xiv) vividly recalls the reality of women's victimization by men in Trinidad:

> street insult and verbal abuse and physical beatings from men; women with scores of children who were forced to beg the 'children's father' for support at his workplace on payday before the money was spent; girls of promise getting pregnant and thereafter losing all the brilliance that they had previously shown, sinking into a round of baby-making for men who saw sex as recreation and women as conquests; all this crowned by an oral culture which endorsed this behaviour.

Likewise, one has only to dip into Sistren's *Lionheart Gal* for evidence of culturally sanctioned brutalization of women on a daily basis in Jamaica. Of course, there are dangers in reading texts simply as 'mirrors' of women's material reality, thus reducing them to sociological documents; none the less, much West Indian fiction by women has political impact because it *does* strike a chord of recognition in female readers.

Again, while post-colonial analyses of West Indian literature would place the 'quest for national identity' that pervaded the canon well into the 1960s within a generalized resistance to hegemonic, imperial discourse, attention to patriarchal oppression elucidates the fact that this concern tended to eclipse issues important to women's writing at the time, thus silencing female voices. For example, Elleke Boehmer (8) points out that 'where, in nationalist rhetoric, as in the official discourse of the state, masculine identity is normative, and where the female is addressed in the main as idealised bearer of nationalist sons [or, as we saw in Chapter 2, as symbol of the nation's glorified African heritage], woman as such, in herself, has no valuable place.'

My point is that it is possible for post-colonial readings to downplay, or ignore, the woman's side of the imperial experience.[1] Therefore I would like to endorse Kathleen Balutansky's observation (forthcoming, 34) that Caribbean women writers 'delineate complex post-colonial *and* feminist positions that offer distinct configurations on the agency of Caribbean women and of the fundamental *complexities* that undermine any attempt to define their identity' (italics mine).

Marlene Nourbese Philip is one writer who engages with post-colonial theory from a feminist perspective. In 'Managing the Unmanageable' (1990: 295) she exposes the centre/margin paradigm of colonial discourse by which European thought designated certain groups – '[w]omen, Africans, Asians and aboriginals' – as both inferior and threatening Other: that is, the 'embodiment of everything which the white male perceived himself not to be'. As post-colonial *woman*, she discusses the difficulty of 'working in a language which traditionally had been yet another tool of oppression' (296), and in her poetry collection (1989), explicitly addresses the task of 'abrogating and appropriating' hegemonic language as part of a woman-centred project. The power of language, and the silencing of the language of the powerless, inform her more recent narrative, *Looking for Livingstone* (1991), as experienced by a female questor.

Is there then, such a thing as 'post-colonial feminist' criticism? W.D. Ashcroft (1989) specifies some areas of overlap between feminism and post-colonialism in the hope that by highlighting cross-fertilizations, 'a greater awareness of each other's strategies may lead to a fusion of energies . . . [and] what has not yet been – a genuine post-colonial feminism' (33).[2] For Ashcroft, both discourses resist authoritarian and neo-authoritarian orthodoxy, and both speak from positions within hegemonic language to subvert it. Both 'woman' and 'post-colonial' exist, to some extent, outside representation itself, in that they are constituted as Other, lack, negation by the dominant discourse. However, he notes the futility of seeking a pre-existing 'authentic' female/national language, free of the taint of patriarchal imperialism, and reiterates Kristeva's assertion that since language is a process, a 'tool for constructing a different reality by initiating different forms of language use' (27), it cannot be imperialist or sexist *per se*, but only in specific articulations.

In addition, Ashcroft considers both discourses to be concerned with writing out of a sense of body/place as colonized, constructed within hegemonic practice, and needing to be revisioned, reconstructed, not in opposition to the patriarchal/imperial norm, but through questioning the binary structuration by which marginalization is justified. His case is a convincing one and, since several of the features he notes complement the strategies of the dub version, I want to subject two texts by West Indian women to a 'post-colonial feminist' reading in this chapter.

However, it is necessary first to address a few of the objections that have been levelled against post-colonial theory. Ketu Katrak (158) deplores the appropriation of literary texts by the 'theory producers and consumers of Western academia', considering that post-colonial theoreticians have succumbed 'to the lure of engaging in a hegemonic discourse of Western theory given that it is "difficult" or "challenging".' But the implication here, that post-colonial theory is a unitary, fixed system, is belied by its very diverse practitioners who themselves argue about the definition of the term. Certainly Ashcroft, Griffiths and Tiffin (155–6) share Katrak's distaste for the reincorporation of literary texts into the hegemonic institutions of 'first world' academia. Further, engaging with 'Western theory', difficult or otherwise, does not seem to me necessarily the kiss of death; indeed, it is part of my purpose in this book since, following the logic of the dub version, I would argue that aspects of *any* theory can quite usefully be appropriated for specific textual analysis. After all, as Laurence Breiner points out (1), at what point does interculturation, the matrix of the much-touted 'plural heritage' of many creole societies, become 'foreign cultural penetration?' In any case, within the Caribbean at least, academic 'patron-age' of post-colonial literary texts generally means economic advantage to the writers as well as a much-needed forum for the dissemination of the frequently subversive ideologies encoded in these texts. For academics in the Caribbean, then, terms like 'appropriation' and 'reincorporation' take on new meanings in regard to 'Western theory'.

Katrak also feels that 'little theoretical production of post-colonial writers [is] given the serious attention it deserves, so that it is dismissed as not theoretical enough by Western standards' (158). Breiner (3) too, considers that post-colonial theory tends to neglect 'indigenous criticism (both contemporary and 'classical'). . . .' In the context of this chapter, I hope to invalidate the latter objection, and as far as Katrak's critique is concerned, in Chapter 4 I cite the engagement with the 'theoretical production of post-colonial writers' by critics like Helen Tiffin, who has discussed Erna Brodber's fiction (1989) and that of Rhys and Naipaul (1992) as *theoretical paradigms.*

Arun Mukherjee (28) is critical of a totalizing tendency in post-colonial theory for, in reading texts solely for anti-colonial resistance, it performs

> several homogenizing functions which produce an essentialized 'na-
> tive' who is devoid of race, gender, class, caste, ethnic, and religious
> markers[;] . . . further . . . that post-colonial theory's exclusive
> concern with this essentialized native's 'resistance' to 'the colonizer',
> another essentialized construction, is politically retrogressive in so far

as it occludes, on the one hand, this resisting native's own ideological agendas and, on the other, the heterogeneity of voices in post-colonial societies.

These are serious reservations and need to be considered in any textual reading: as Breiner notes (3), 'we need to be wary of theory – and of our own theorizing – to the extent that it constitutes a standardized managerial structure, imported from the centre, [and] imposed in a variety of settings. . . .' However, he also concedes that 'post-colonial theory doesn't have to be a monolithic theory, always global in application' but might be 'a battery of techniques and reliable nomenclatures that enable us to make sense of what can be found . . . among the many situations that are "post-colonial"' (4).

Further, the strategic focus of reading for resistance privileged in post-colonial theory does not imply 'that nothing else takes place at the level of post-colonial literary expression' (Slemon, 1992: 8). Ashcroft, Griffiths and Tiffin appear to hold, with Lyotard (166), that as far as their project goes, the intention is not to substitute a new monolithic critical discourse in the place of imperialism, but rather 'to articulate a weave of practices grounded in the particular and the local.' Theoretical concern for textual resistance to colonial interpellation, is but one of several possible politically motivated analytical choices. Certainly, Katrak has clear notions as to theory's political engagement: '[s]ocial responsibility must be the basis of any theorizing on post-colonial literature as well as the root of the creative work of the writers themselves' (157). A mite prescriptive, perhaps, as far as the 'creative work' goes, but the sentiment is shared by post-colonial theorist Slemon (1992: 3) for whom this approach, 'first and foremost, is a commitment to anti-colonialist critical *work* at the level of research and teaching – in other words, it is the name for a method of reading, and the name for a *kind* of commitment towards the production of social change.' It seems to me that 'theory' in the West Indian context is less an intellectual 'game' than part of a political practice.

Of course, I have been unfair to the above-mentioned critics, whose problems with aspects of post-colonial theory I have not been able fully to contextualize; further, I have only addressed their comments in so far as they relate to West Indian literature, which is *my* focus but not entirely theirs. It is not my purpose here to represent the debate in its entirety, but simply to point to certain reservations about wholesale adoption of this, as of any, theory, in analyzing a specific body of texts. Indeed, I want to keep Mukherjee's stricture – that the notion of a post-colonial essence 'supposedly shared by geographically dispersed and historically, culturally, linguistically, politically, and racially different societies and the texts produced by their members' (29) is, to put it mildly, problematic – very much in mind. However, although I want to attend with Mukherjee (30) to 'fundamental differences within particular national formations – differences, let us say, of class, or of gender formation,' I do think that a combination of strategies 'lifted' from post-colonial *and* feminist theories can usefully underline the heterogeneity of West Indian texts by women that enables the transcendence of limiting patriarchal/imperial structures. A reading of Kincaid's *Annie John* and Brodber's *Jane and Louisa*, as articulating post-colonial feminist impulses, may prove illustrative.

Annie John: Reconsidering **Paradise Lost**

Imperial and patriarchal discourse, as Ashcroft observes, often overlap. One example is the female embodiment in mythology of a fabulous, unspoilt 'virgin' territory that awaits European civilization. The perennial Caribbean myth of El Dorado was variously articulated in imperial writings as a virgin awaiting ravishment, a sleeping princess requiring the male touch to awake, and so on.

But West Indian women writers also image the native place as female. Michelle Cliff (1990: 266) has said that she understands the landscape of her native Jamaica as 'female' largely because 'the land is redolent of my grandmother and mother.' The 'conquest' factor is absent here. Indeed, Lemuel Johnson (128ff) discusses Cliff's fiction as calling woman's body into question within and *against* such 'conquest of America' paradigms. For Marlene Nourbese Philip (1991: 61) the penetration of the African continent as sexual penetration of the female is part of Livingstone's (patriarchal/imperial) discourse. Fido (1991: 347) adds another dimension when she cites Kristeva's association of the Mother as lost country, as paradise lost, in the female imaginary.

Annie John draws together these associations – native land/Mother/ paradisal Eden/ravished 'virgin' territory – and complicates their interactions. The story turns on Annie's relationship with her mother (and with colonial Antigua): initially a close and sensual symbiosis, imaged as Eden ('It was in such a paradise that I lived' (25)), the relationship becomes problematic, Annie suffers the loss of paradise and the rest of the narrative depicts her resulting emotional trauma until her departure from mother and motherland.

The loss of paradise is an inevitable outcome within the myths of El Dorado. Such Edens *must* enter the 'real world', in imperial discourse, via the penetration of the colonizer, the representative of reason and faith who brings enlightenment to the 'dark continent'. By analogy, woman cannot *become* woman without losing her virginity, having her body colonized by the male; or, in Lacanian terms, entering the Symbolic Order and accommodating herself to the Law of the Father (patriarchy).

In all versions of the myth, conquest brings about a loss of innocence, a fall from pre-Columbian grace – in *Paradise Lost* (9; 1115–8), Milton explicitly links America before Columbus with pre-lapsarian Eden – which is accompanied, regretfully, by corruption, as sin and mortality enter the world. Yet by some twist of logic, it is not the despoiling conquistador, the phallic serpent in the garden who gets the blame. With the incorporation of the Judeo-Christian story of the Fall into mythical representations of the loss of unspoilt El Dorado, it is the woman who becomes responsible. Paradise is lost through Eve's sin; sin and death enter the world when Pandora opens her box. The phallic serpent may be the catalyst, but a She was 'asking for it'. And this holds true for *Annie John*. Here, the fall from grace that is so movingly evoked – a theme which, Leslie Garis (70) claims, haunts *all* Kincaid's work – is initiated by the mother.

Milton's epic informs *Annie John* on several levels. For her irreverent commentary on imperial history (defacing a picture of Columbus in her textbook), Annie's punishment is to copy out Books I and II of *Paradise Lost* (82). Post-colonial disobedience is treated by the forced assimilation of large doses of a canonical work that, significantly, inscribes woman as narcissistic, greedy, weak and credulous, ambitious and essentially inferior to man.[3] Annie is to learn what befalls women *and* natives who resist the inferior roles allotted them.

In a sense, *Annie John* can be read as a localized version of *Paradise Lost*, but one which subtly reworks the ideological foundations of Milton's classic. For Annie does not learn her lesson. Instead, she identifies with another marginalized player in the myth, with Lucifer, whose exile from and plotted revenge against heaven form the subject of Books I and II of *Paradise Lost*. Seeing her black female body reflected in a shop window, Annie notes similarities with a picture of 'The Young Lucifer', a depiction of 'Satan just recently cast out of heaven for all his bad deeds . . . standing on a black rock all alone and naked' (94). Like Cathy in *Wuthering Heights*, Annie reconciles herself to hell rather than live in a heaven where, as native/ woman, she must acquiesce in her subservience. Interestingly, in Kincaid's subsequent novel *Lucy*, the eponymous heroine *rejoices* in the association with Satan:

> Lucy, a girl's name for Lucifer. That my mother would have found me devil-like did not surprise me, for I often thought of her as god-like, and are not the children of gods devils? . . . whenever I saw my name I always reached out to give it a strong embrace. (153)

To return to the implicit textual link of mother as Eve: in one sense, *Annie John* indicts the mother for her sin of collusion in imperial and patriarchal subjection of women. The snake carried unwittingly on the mother's head along with her load of fruit (68–69), is symbolic of both the colonial ethos she has internalized and determines to pass on to her daughter,[4] and 'the young lady business' (female decorum, domesticity and subservience) into which she tries to educate Annie; Abruna (1991: 281ff) goes into some detail on this subject. The mother is, for Annie, a 'serpent' (52) because she is the agent of female socialization which Cooper (1991: 68) explains as carrying 'the burdens of generalized respectability, but more the gender-specific weight of appropriate behaviour for an upright young woman in colonial [Antigua]. . . .'

As a 'post-colonial feminist' project, then, *Annie John* rejects the mother as a servant of *both* Mother Country and patriarchy; similarly, *Wide Sargasso Sea* conflates Antoinette's husband's roles as British colonizer *and* agent of male domination. It is significant that during her mysterious illness/breakdown, Annie launders family photographs, erasing all that is *white* except for a pair of shoes she insisted on wearing, despite her mother's injunction against them: 'not fit for a *young lady* and not fit for wearing or being received into church' (119) [italics mine].

Donna Perry argues that Annie looks to an alternative mother figure, Ma Chess, to counteract her mother's influence. For Perry, Annie utilizes indigenous woman-centred arts (obeah, story-telling) as empowering sources in writing her *own* life against the increasingly repulsive version her mother has prepared for her. As do many post-colonial texts, *Annie John* dismantles the 'rightness' of the centre/margin paradigm in looking beyond the colonized mother to the alter/native wisdom of the grandmother who represents here – as in *Crick Crack Monkey*, *No Telephone to Heaven* and Maryse Condé's *La Vie Scélérate* – non-European resources.[5]

There is another sense in which the novel engages with *Paradise Lost*, particularly the representation of mother as Eve, and this has to do with female sexuality. In Milton's epic, Eve's sin is followed almost immediately by carnal knowledge, an account of lust-inflamed intercourse (9; 1013–16). The consequent shame and guilt surrounding the sexual act and the body (9; 1058) are blamed by God (10; 192–208) and Adam, on the woman. 'Thus it shall befall/Him who, to worth in women overtrusting,/ Lets her will rule' (9; 1182–84). Female sexuality is shameful and brings death into the world.

Addressing the Second International Conference of Caribbean Women Writers, Sylvia Wynter (1990b) pointed out that creation myths tend to mark women with negative symbols: for example, associating the downward flow of menstrual blood with the sublunary world, the province of mortality, is to link woman's physicality with mutability (a mark of sinfulness) and death. Of course, she noted, blacks were also associated with the degraded earth in Eurocentric evaluations. Wynter's point was that *all* knowledge encodes gender, and racial, constructs; myths articulate ideologies, not universal truths. Thus, within Judeo-Christian discourse, woman is to mutable nature and death as man is to culture and life, and this *justifies* the inferior placing of women. Once the code is secularized, such 'natural' inferiority also accounts for women's economic and social inequality.

Annie John (and Brodber's *Jane and Louisa Will Soon Come Home*) focuses on these associations, by examining the repercussions on the female child of the woman/sexuality/death construct. At puberty, Nellie experiences bodily changes as marks of sin: 'I have the devil in me' (*Jane and Louisa*, 122). As noted above, it is in contemplating her developing body that Annie makes her identification with Lucifer. To be sexual woman is to be in a fallen state. Hence, Nellie accepts that she must be 'shipped out' of the paradisal garden of childhood for 'cleansing', and then 'preserved like peppers in a kilner jar' (122) by Aunt Becca: that is, learn to 'bottle up' her sexuality. Annie too learns, from her mother, that to grow to womanhood is, very likely, to become a 'slut' (102), a dirty, shameful fate.

By contrast, the relatively ungendered childhood condition is paradisal: pre-pubescent femaleness is perfection. Helen Pyne-Timothy refers to the early mother/daughter relationship in *Annie John* in terms of Nancy Chodorow's description of the pre-Oedipal dyad: mother and daughter lovingly reflect each other's perfection, and the father is, at best, peripheral. At puberty, however, bodily changes ('small tufts of hair had appeared under my arms, and when I perspired the smell was strange, as if I had turned into a strange animal' (25)) coincide with maternal rejection, expulsion from paradise. The message is clear in both novels: 'It', as Nellie terms female sexuality, completely redetermines how one is seen. 'It' constructs woman as body, but body signifying the fallen state, something to be ashamed of and hidden away. 'It' is a mark of sin, hence the enforced separation of Annie from her sensual identification with the mother's body, to which the father now makes his 'rightful' claim.

For Annie, the crisis comes when – significantly, returning from Sunday School – she witnesses her parents making love. Her focus on the mother's hand caressing her father's back, a hand that 'was white and bony, as if it had long been dead and had been left out in the elements' (30) completes the equation: woman + sexuality = fall = death. Perhaps, however, 'equation' is the wrong term for the complex of associations in the young girl's consciousness. Whatever the logic, from this moment on, adult heterosexuality (embodied parentally) evokes utter disgust; at one stage, Annie erases photographs of her parents 'from the waist down' (120).

The intrusion of the male is a betrayal of the female dyad: hence Annie's horror at her friend Gwen's suggestion that Annie will marry her brother (93). And again, Annie's mother is to blame, for she, like Eve has abandoned the pre-Oedipal paradise and *chosen* her 'fall' into sexuality. So, when confronted with her mother's accusation of being a slut, Annie replies, accurately enough, 'like mother like daughter' (102).[6] In addition, she blames her mother for the *consequences* of the fall, the sentence handed down for the female sin of sexuality: that is, wifely submission *(Paradise Lost,* 10; 195–6: 'to thy husband's will/Thine shall submit; he over thee shall rule'). Her god-like mother, who defied paternal tyranny, is now seen to enjoy the servile state *vis-à-vis* her husband. Worse, mother/Eve insists on the same fate for her daughter! Since, as Pyne-Timothy (238) observes, Annie's mother has suppressed her female (hetero)sexuality in her role-modelling – like many West Indian mothers, she seems to see this as a source of shame[7] – her sudden recommendation of marriage and mother-hood to Annie is shocking, and categorically rejected as absurd.

Finally, mother/Eve is associated with death. In her fallen, subordi-nate state, she is dead to Annie and, in that she has ostensibly cast her daughter out of their symbiotic childhood paradise, she brings about the death of that earlier Annie. Forced into awareness of her sexuality and the gender-linked oppression 'It' entails, Annie is bitterly aware of her loss; of the freedom, power and security of the undifferentiated self-with-mother, the Edenic state, which she once enjoyed. Hence, the novel is suffused with nostalgia and longing for what Bryant Magnum (259) terms 'the wholeness and completeness that characterize the harmonious prelapsarian world.'

In keeping with Mukherjee's call (30) for attention to fundamental differences *within* particular national formations in post-colonial texts, I have tried to demonstrate that the conflict in *Annie John* between native woman and patriarchal/imperial ideology takes place in the heart of the 'native' family. Like *Beka Lamb*, Kincaid's novel treats one family as a microcosm of conflicting gender and class orientations in the wider society. Certainly, the school plays a role in ideological transmission. The 'young lady business' is a class-based construct ('lady' rather than 'woman') which, as noted in Chapter 2, was engrained in the colonial education girls received in the West Indies. As Katrak (171) explains, 'female education, governed by Victorian ideology and Christian missionary zeal, was aimed at produc-ing women as good wives and mothers.' In both *Annie John* and *Jane and Louisa Will Soon Come Home,* this is also the aim of the older women in the family circle with respect to the girl children in their care.

Kincaid's text portrays Annie coming into being as 'Annie John' – one who knows her 'true true name' – a subject who resists hegemonic definitions of colonial/woman on *all* fronts. In addition to rejecting what her mother stands for, Donna Perry points out that Annie also rejects represen-tations of black people in school books *and* images of women in canonical tests such as *Jane Eyre* and *Paradise Lost.* Annie demands her *own* trunk, her *own* story.

Giovanna Covi (353) situates Kincaid's writing in the best tradition of the dub version when she claims 'it challenges any possibility of deciphering a single meaning by emphasizing multiplicity.' However, within this multiplicity, Covi acknowledges that

> [t]he main theme of her writings is the inquiry into the feminine role and racial difference. Kincaid criticizes the very existence of sexual and racial difference, rather than the modes of their existence (346–7)

Annie John demonstrates the construction of colonial woman within imperial and patriarchal discourse, *and* disrupts the hegemony of such discourse by questioning its assumptions, particularly the flawed reasoning of Western mythology as expressed in *Paradise Lost*. Refusing the idea that women's sexuality is rooted in sin and results in death, *Annie John* suggests that acquiescing in patriarchy, accepting the Law of the Father (becoming gendered as inferior Other), results in the death of female subjectivity and agency.

Additionally, with the multiple focus of the dub version, the novel conflates female Othering with colonial Othering. In appropriating myths that construct woman/native in certain pejorative ways, the post-colonial feminist text regains some measure of control over them; in querying their constructions, it undermines their ideological power. Finally, by locating themselves in the specifically West Indian context, such texts demonstrate how contending discourses – Olive Senior's 'The Two Grandmothers', in her 1989 collection, is a wonderful example – problematize women's self-definitions in the region. And it is this issue of contending discourses that I want to address in the rest of this chapter.

Jane and Louisa Will Soon Come Home: cast out of the 'beautiful garden'

For the female protagonists of *Annie John* and *Jane and Louisa* and, incidentally, Margaret Atwood's *Cat's Eye* (1989), childhood evokes images of warmth, security, belonging; it is represented textually, in Earl Ingersoll's terms (20), as 'a paradise lost of relatively ungendered life as a child in nature.' For Elaine in *Cat's Eye* and Nellie in Brodber's novel, the loss of the 'beautiful garden' coincides with a forced encounter with their 'femaleness' as socially determined. And, with Annie, Nellie's socialization into adulthood is a complex initiation into hierarchies of race and class, as well as gender.

Jane and Louisa opens with a delineation of Nellie's ancestry, with its apparently polarized referents:

> Papa's grandfather and Mama's mother were the upper reaches of our world. So we were brown, intellectual, better and apart, two genera-

tions of lightening blue-blacks and gracing elementary schools with brightness. The cream of the earth, isolated, quadroon, mulatto, Anglican. But we had two wiry black hands up to the elbows in khaki suds . . .(7)

'Papa's grandfather' was the white ancestor, whose legacy includes 'principle, invisible gifts of daffodils . . . Hamletian castles and wafer disintegrating on your tongue' (30): that is, gentlemanly behaviour, English literature and high Church of England allegiance. 'Mama's mother' Granny Tucker, is proudly black, Baptist and the epitome of rural respectability. Her legacy also includes denial of her slave antecedents (31) and repression of her husband's anti-imperialist anger. From these forebears come the 'new generation' of which Nellie is a part; brown-skinned, middle class, educated, Anglican, well-spoken and distanced from the black and the poor, 'those people so different – different from us' (73) who 'throw dice, slam dominoes and give-laugh-for-peasoup all day long. They have no culture, no sense of identity, no shame or respect for themselves' (51).

Again, Nellie's family history offers a range of female role models. There is Tia Maria, self-effacing black great-grandmother; Aunt Alice, eccentric to the point of craziness, silent, unmarried and cheerfully without responsibility; Aunt Becca, middle class and proper, who made a 'good' marriage at the cost of aborting her illegitimate child. Contrasting with Aunt Becca's barrenness are the mysterious cousins B, Teena and Letitia, 'fallen' women who 'had simply dropped [their children] U-roy and Locksley and Obadiah and vanished into the crowd' (143). To Nellie, these initiates into 'It' (female sexuality) represent power – the luxury toys they send back for their children – *and* the terrifying propensity of the womb to become a scrap-heap, a devalued dumping ground for unwanted and unplanned children. Obviously, the commodification of the womb has terrible resonances for the descendants of slave women in the Caribbean.

This fear and shame associated with female sexuality informs Nellie's mother's construction of physical development as a 'hidey-hidey' thing. 'You are eleven now,' she tells her daughter, 'and soon something strange will happen to you' (23). And this strange something changes Nellie, sets her (like Annie John) apart as tainted, defiled: 'So I am different. Something is wrong with me' (23). For respectable Aunt Becca, female sexuality, and its attendant vulnerability, is to be repressed: 'save yourself lest you turn woman before your time' (17). On the other hand, a different ethos faces Nellie at university, urging sexual liberation:

> You want to be a woman; now you have a man, you'll be like everybody else. You're normal now! Vomit and bear it. (28)

Another alternative is to ignore the whole sordid issue of female sexuality and adopt the mask of the cerebral intellectual woman, the committed student of progressive thought: the emotionally sterile 'cracked doll' *kumbla* that Nellie assumes for a time. From the bewildering range of roles and hierarchical alliances in her society, Nellie is taught to use sexual repression and social exclusiveness as defences against 'those people' who 'will drag you down' (17) if they can.

But the novel also dramatizes the *cost* of being so rigidly classed and gendered, through the representation of Nellie's fragmentation and collapse. Brodber (1982; 1990) has explained that *Jane and Louisa* originated as a therapeutic exercise, a case study of the 'dissociative personality' for her abnormal psychology students in Jamaica. In addition to the dub version's lack of respect for 'coherence', this accounts for the initially fractured narrative structure, which begins to 'come together' as the putative 'patient' re-lives the traumatic events which led to psychic collapse, and begins the reconstructive process. Thus, as Nellie 'reconnects' herself, the narrative operates like a 'moving camera' film, coherently relating the familial and social history that has produced her. As Brodber (1982) explains,

> if someone is going to give you the moving picture, they are going to give you the whole of your past and you are just going to have to look at it and deal with it. By the end, it is a complete picture – when the patient has been able to cope and has been able to see that something has to happen, and a new life has to be forged out of the past.

Textually, then, *Jane and Louisa* evokes a personality, indeed a society, fragmented by contending discourses. For Nellie, as for Tee in *Crick Crack Monkey* (62),

> doubleness, or this particular kind of doubleness, was a thing to be taken for granted. Why, the whole of life was like a piece of cloth, with a right side and a wrong side.

Hutcheon (161–2) has noted the sense of duality which marks the colonial, and it is to such 'doubleness' that Brodber (1990: 165) refers in describing imperial discourse in post-Independence Jamaica as 'a ghost that talked through black faces'. Further, this notion of doubleness, of contending discourses is reflected in the novel's complex web of linguistic variation.

In *Jane and Louisa*, several communities interact, each with its own cultural agenda and related set of linguistic patterns. One line of Nellie's ancestry operates according to a set of values inherent in the insistence upon using 'the Queen's English', the language of the educated, upwardly mobile. Another is comfortable using Jamaican Creole, the language of the majority of black, partially-educated working-class Jamaicans. But these speech communities, as represented in the text, should not be seen as

evidence of a simple bilingualism. Jamaican Creole is not one homogeneous system, the province of the 'folk', but a complex of styles and registers
into which *all* speakers fit at some point or other. 'Standard' English may
be hegemonic, but is constantly 'interfered with' by non-standard lects in
the West Indian situation. A wonderful example, used to great comic and
ideologically subversive effect, occurs in Samuel Selvon's 1975 novel,
Moses Ascending where Moses' attempt to write the polished, literary
English he valorizes, is consistently sabotaged by his own Creole register
which undercuts the imperial hegemony he wants to articulate.

Most linguists agree that what operates in Jamaica is a language
continuum ranging from acrolect (Jamaican standard English) through to
basilect ('broad' Creole), with intermediate (mesolectal) registers; speakers
'code shift' or 'style range' along the spectrum according to their linguistic
range of competence,[8] and according to the social context of the speech
situation. Code-switching within the continuum is a matter of performance,
of behavioural realization, since one's speech is often an important indication of membership in a certain ethnic, occupational, age or peer group, of
one's class or level of education. So shifting from one lect to another
implies shifting social positions. Thus Nellie, in the bosom of her rural
family, uses a mesolectal variety of Creole nearer to the basilect:

> But is not me one frighten. Everybody else frighten too and they
> quiet, quiet, when my father stop talking. (14)

But Nellie, the grown up and 'citified' schoolgirl, speaking to her
middle-class Aunt Becca (with whom she is on less intimate terms), switches
to a more acrolectal register:

> But I am sixteen, a prefect at school and a patrol leader. You let me
> go on hikes. You let me go to evensong and speech festival by myself
> at night. I don't understand. (16)

And later, the adult Nellie slips from her careful, educated speech into
nearly basilectal Creole, in the heat of her anger at Baba:

> You understand this damn shameless rasta-man who is to tell me that
> he wants to watch me grow. You understand this r . . . -c . . . t of a
> hungry man from nowhere who is to watch and observe me. What the
> hell he think he is. Man don't let me. . . . (71)

Speakers, then, are very rarely limited to one lect and, particularly in
the urban environment where social mobility and class interaction are more
common, verbal adaptability is a useful skill. I would also stress the connection between code-switching and role playing here. Tia's advice to her
'khaki' (mixed race) children concerning their language – '[y]ou mustn't
say bway, you must say bai. Talk like your father' (138) – is an injunction

to identify themselves with his privileged status. Assumption of identity through choice of speech register is a valuable camouflage. This is reflected in the novel (123–30) in the parable of Anancy's escape from Dryhead's kingdom through role playing via language. Assuming the pose of a humble, broken man, who has no option but to deliver his children to the tyrant, Anancy says

> I broke, I los', I bow to you. You is King. I just can't make it, can't mek it at all. I bring the children them. All of them. (125–6)

He has been caught poaching, but explains away the fishy smell in his boat as the result of his heartbroken children overturning it in an attempt to stop their father.

And, verbally gifted as he is, Anancy is quick to seize on and manipulate the weaknesses of others: Firefly's inability to distinguish linguistically between singular and plural tense means that he is confused visually also, as to whether Anancy has brought one child or many. This leads to Anancy's master-stroke: the double meaning behind his public vilification of his child/children, 'Go eena kumbla.'

> To Dryhead and his court, this was a bad word that only a man so torn with grief could utter to his child. To Tacuma, it meant: find yourself a camouflage and get back into the store house. (128)

Purely by playing a certain role and by linguistic skill, Anancy manages to erect a deceptive facade for his captors, and then to escape through it.

The manifestations of 'doubleness' – code-switching, role playing, the assumption of camouflages (*kumblas*) are central to Brodber's text, and essential survival strategies for Nellie. But choosing one model or role of 'femaleness' necessitates a denial of other aspects of womanhood, to the detriment of self-integration; whereas the cousins are imaged as womb at the expense of intellect, the 'cracked doll' is head without connection to sexual body. Competing linguistic registers reflect the complex of race, class and gender options with which Nellie must grapple – a kind of 'multiple choice' life test.

For a time she retreats from it all into her *kumbla* but, as previously noted, this is temporary. Nellie's emergence involves recognition that in her creole society, multiplicity is integral and she *need not* choose between polarized gender, class or racial extremes. Psychic and emotional reintegration – becoming 'a walking-talking human being' instead of a role-playing zombie – necessitates acceptance of her plural heritage. Again, by refusing genre boundaries and moving fluidly between speech registers and literary styles, the form of Brodber's text implicitly encodes this regenerative strategy.

So, when Nellie screams Creole expletives at him, Baba congratulates her on having found her language (having recuperated that part of the continuum previously repressed in her playing out the role scripted for her) and says,

> Next thing you'll be telling me where I come from and that would really be telling as you know. (71)

There is double meaning here too. To tell someone where they come from, is part of the abusive ritual of 'tracing' in Jamaica, as elsewhere in the Caribbean, entailing graphic, and insulting, description of sexual origin. For Nellie to 'come down to this level', to reacknowledge the earthy aspect of sexuality in general and her own in particular, is something of a break-through in the 'coming together' of her dissociated self. Additionally, Baba's statement operates on the more standard level and, in the final section of the novel, Nellie *does* tell, of her and Baba's shared origins, where they come from, what and who has made her - *all* of which she must acknowledge. As Brodber (1982) explains,

> you have to know them (the ancestors) and you have to know that these were the problems and this was how they dealt with them; you have to know that this was how the women of your past, of your race or of your nation have dealt with it, and you have to look and you have to shake their hands still and know that this was their way of coping. But it does not necessarily mean that you have to do it this way.

Like the dub version, *Jane and Louisa* recommends and demonstrates the need for exploring all options yet refusing to be bound by any one definition; in post-colonial terms, it refuses the binary oppositions within which the colonial subject was written, and insists on the acknowledgement of indigenous heterogeneity and plurality – a context which may fragment the subject, but out of which creative futures can be made. In the end, the text articulates a political theory: tolerance, even espousal of the continuum – of language/gender roles/ancestral affiliation – is necessary to meaningful representation of a creole reality. Nellie may, of course, choose to identify for a time with one 'register' rather than another, but acknowledging that she is the product of *all*, that her heritage is indubitably as hybrid as Jamaican Creole, is her key discovery *and* the source of her new strength. Carolyn Cooper (1990: 280) considers that Brodber's use of 'the central framing device of the creolized English quadrille dance, and the children's ring game derived from it' (the 'Jane and Louisa will soon come home' refrain of this game gives the novel its title) suggests 'the adaptive capacity of neo-African folk culture in Jamaica, its conscription of English folk traditions for its own enrichment: fiddling with their dance!' This is typical post-colonial dub version appropriation.

Other West Indian women writers explicitly note the coexistence of dual or, more accurately, multiple traditions at the source of their creativity.

Lorna Goodison (1990: 290) feels that the 'double language, which is part of my [Jamaican] heritage, is one of the main influences on my work. . . .' Similarly, Michelle Cliff (1990: 264) speaks of 'inventing my own peculiar speech, one that attempts to draw together everything I am and have been, both Caliban and Ariel and a liberated and synthesized version of each.' The urge to multiplicity, to replacing notions of 'our language' versus 'their language' with recognition of a range of linguistic and cultural options right here at home, seems to be widespread among Caribbean women writers.

This is not to propose that the debate over which variant is 'authentic' for literary representation – a debate begun over twenty years ago – does not concern them. Interestingly, a writer like Marlene Nourbese Philip, long resident in North America, sometimes theorizes within the old binary opposition of the colonizer's alien language as against an indigenous creative alternative. Others refuse to *recognize* a standard code but emphasize, as does Jean D'Costa (1990: 259) the 'fusion of differing linguistic and generic codes . . . [as] the primary challenge to the new writer.' Pollard (1991) is particularly astute in demonstrating how exploitation of linguistic tensions in West Indian texts by women serves to dramatize the variant social and cultural determinants, the 'contending discourses' at work in their societies. A careful study of how her own fiction and poetry enact this variation to telling effect, is already overdue.

Thus, positions *vis-à-vis* the very meaning of 'language' in the postcolonial Caribbean are healthily plural; the same goes for the continuing 'oral/scribal' debate in women's writing within the region.[9] And, as noted, in the fiction a playful irreverence operates with respect to variation. If, as Ashcroft, Griffiths and Tiffin maintain, '[i]n writing out of the condition of "Otherness", post-colonial texts assert the complex of intersecting "peripheries" as the actual substance of experience' (78), I would argue that such a perspective is even more integral to reading West Indian female-authored fictions.

Returning briefly to *Jane and Louisa*: a sense of community pervades the novel, with family, friends, neighbours and ancestors cohering into an almost tangible speaking presence:

> Dearie and Sister, Sweet Boy and Girlie and all of us mouth; the voice belongs to the family group dead and alive. (12)

As noted, the community can be supportive or malicious (112); although Nellie's fractured state is a result of conflicting discourses within this community, it is only through the group that her healing will be possible. The novel details her engineering of an active self through reconstruction of communal past, hence Nellie's conclusion:

> I had to know them to know what I was about; that I could no how wear my rightful Easter dress, sit in my granny's parlour, eat my cane

nor walk in my beautiful garden unless I walked with them, the black and squat, the thin and wizened, all of them. (80)

Brodber herself (1982), in what I would call a feminist orientation since it links personal and political therapy, argues that

> I'm making the same claim for the history of the nation – that you have to go back and look at it, no matter how distressing, no matter how dirty, no matter how your myths have to be destroyed, you still have to go back and look at it. And when you finish, you have to decide whether you're going to live with it, whether you're going to forget it, or – hopefully – you say, well it's so it go and let me do my piece and claim it.

In other words, Nellie has to re-read her history, confronting negative as well as positive constituents, and accept the entire *blend*. As Joyce Walker-Johnson points out (49), the two distinct traditions with which the novel opens ('Papa's grandfather' and 'Mama's mother') quickly cross-fertilize through Nellie's parents; differing races, classes, gender roles, religious affiliations, linguistic practices and political strategies achieve an (initially problematic) synthesis in Nellie herself, as in her country.

The final section of the novel reiterates its opening image of a 'mossy covert dim and dark', a secure world as warm and safe as eggs under a hen. From this 'relatively ungendered' childhood, Nellie – like Annie John – is expelled. *Jane and Louisa* concludes with a clearing of paths leading out of the beautiful garden; *Annie John* closes with a voyage to new shores.[10] In a sense, the young women *cannot* become such without losing paradise; and yet there is a subdued optimism at the end of both narratives, contrasting with the tragic tone of *Paradise Lost*, because they have chosen to construct their own womanhood.

The two novels 'unpack' contending stereotypes of femininity, of race and class fixity, within which female socialization frequently occurred in the colonial and post-colonial West Indies.[11] Further, the texts explore the complex nature of this socialization by attending to conflicting discourses *within* the indigenous group (family/community) responsible for the girl child.

Yet the novels also question privileged 'master narratives' and challenge their construction of the colonial female within, for example, certain myths. They refuse narrow options based on polarities and instead embrace a (creole) principle of plurality that, we might say, theoretically renders *invalid* concepts of marginalization. In the process, they inscribe complex post-colonial women protagonists who represent, in Mukherjee's terminology (33), 'subjects in their own right whose subjectivity is composed of many other things beside their relationship, both past and present, with "the

colonizer".' As such, *Annie John* and *Jane and Louisa Will Soon Come
Home* can be read instructively as post-colonial feminist 'woman versions'
of West Indian fiction.

Notes

1   This is the point of Bev Brown's 'Mansong and Matrix: A Radical Experi-
     ment' (1986). Brown takes Edward Kamau Brathwaite's post-colonial prac-
     tice to task for being 'male-centred and inadequate for interpreting writing
     by Caribbean women' (68). Instead, she considers Zee Edgell's *Beka Lamb*
     as holding the key to 'an emerging woman-centred colonization/adaptation
     theory [which] allows women to voice what remains silent in the holes of
     Brathwaite's discourse' (68). It is also possible for feminist readings to
     downplay, or ignore, the role of imperialism in the construction of woman,
     as Spivak (1985) points out with reference to analyses of *Jane Eyre* and *Wide
     Sargasso Sea.*
2   I would maintain that since Ashcroft wrote this article, if not before, some
     critics have been evolving such an approach; several of the essays in Davies
     and Fido (eds) (1990), for example, evidence a post-colonial and feminist
     critical orientation.
3   See, for example, Book IV: 440–8 (Eve's secondary state); 460–8 (her
     narcissism); Book IX: 733–4 (her credulity); 740–3 and 791–3 (her greed
     and over-indulgence); 815–25 (her cunning and ambitious nature); 877–8
     (her deceit); 1059–63 (linked with other temptresses).
4   In an interview with Selwyn Cudjoe (1990), Kincaid expressed the view that
     her mother was formerly an 'Anglophile' and explained that 'the way I am
     is solely owing to her. I was always being told I should be something, and
     then my whole upbringing was something I was not: it was English' (219).
     Like Antoinette in *Wide Sargasso Sea*, Annie is trained to be 'an English
     girl' in the tropics.
5   On this subject, see Anthea Morrison (1990) and Michelle Cliff (1990:
     266–68). Grandmothers represent women with important spiritual and social
     skills – beyond those associated with the vocation of wife and mother – in a
     number of Caribbean texts by women, in which they link granddaughters to
     traditions that balance those of the mother/Mother Country.
6   Note Annie's awareness (113) of her fathers maleness and her sexual arousal
     while sitting on his lap. Again, daughter identifies with mother in this
     shameful, 'sluttish' sexuality. In *Lucy*, Lucy is an Eve figure herself, con-
     fronting her god-like mother (94) and asserting her 'sluttish' sexuality (129).
7   Hazel Carby's comment on Nella Larsen (174) may shed some light on this,
     despite the specifically Afro-American context. Carby maintains that Larsen
     recognized 'the repression of the sensual' [in female socialization] was in
     reaction 'to the long history of the exploitation of black sexuality', which
     'led to the repression of passion and the repression or denial of female
     sexuality and desire.' Certainly, in *Jane and Louisa Will Soon Come Home*
     the wish to protect girl children from male exploitation of their sexuality,
     with its resulting entrapment in unwanted pregnancy and economic depend-
     ency, motivates a harsh insistence on 'virtue' and the censure of desire in
     young women.

Note also Laura Niesen de Abruna (1991: 282) on Annie's mother's 'belief in the necessity of guarding one's sexual virtue if one is to be an unspoiled commodity on the marriage market.' Abruna thinks Annie's mother 'believes that a woman's body is the property of a respectable male who will marry her' (281). Until then, strict vigilance over that body is a necessary part of a mother's role.

Finally, see Isabel Carrera Suarez (1991: 297) who argues that female characters in Joan Riley's fiction view the female body through a male gaze: as objects of violation. Hence, her characters, like Annie and Nellie, reject their new physical development; they do not wish to grow to womanhood because of the innate vulnerability of 'the female sexual/social role.'

8   See David De Camp (13–19) and Mervyn Alleyne (8).
9   See, for example, Carolyn Cooper (1989: 49–57) on narrative form in Sistren's *Lionheart Gal*. Cooper's experimental theorizing *in* Jamaican Creole is itself a significant input into the discussion.
10   In her subsequent novel, *Lucy*, Kincaid represents the young girl's journey from her Caribbean island to the metropolis as a (reverse) re-enactment of Columbus's voyage of discovery and conquest. Kincaid's post-colonial re-writing of this archetypal voyage of Empire is analyzed by Ledent and King-Aribisala in their provocative papers.
11   See Betty Wilson (1991) for a study of this socialization in 'literature and life'. *Lionheart Gal* explores this issue at length.

CHAPTER 4 | Engineering female subjectivity

The last three chapters have attempted to sketch the ways in which the figure of the colonized female in the West Indies has been doubly marginalized, constituting a paradoxical subject without agency, without power. As noted, literary explorations of this state range from depiction of alienation (Chapter 1) to psychic fragmentation (Chapter 2). Chapter 3 discussed literary representations of the colonial female subject whose own self-image is very much at odds with those offered by her society; but the texts mentioned also embody the possibility of refusing such imposed stereotypes/images and appropriating/rewriting myths that have long articulated and justified female alterity. Accordingly, it is possible to recuperate or to engineer a female subjectivity that *is* empowered, that *has* agency.

Brodber's second novel, *Myal*, as well as Hodge's *Crick Crack Monkey* demonstrate how colonial woman has been written in a certain way, 'consolidated' within the texts of colonial education, and how the confrontation of colonized female with this fixed 'Otherness' leads to trauma. The education system put in place by the British in the West Indies has, as noted, been the subject of literary attack from the earliest days of regional writing. It has also come under scrutiny from post-colonial theorists. Tiffin (1989a) argues that the constitution of Caribbean 'Other' in European textuality (29) informed the social or civilizing mission of imperialism, in which education was complicit. Slemon (1987: 7) clarifies this involvement:

> one of colonialism's most salient technologies for social containment and control is the circulation within colonial cultures of the canonical European literary text. Mediated through the colonialist educational apparatus, the European literary text becomes a powerful machinery for forging what Gramsci called cultural domination by consent. . . .

Works such as *The Tempest* or *Robinson Crusoe*, which Tiffin terms 'the classic formulations of Europe's encounters with alterity', were used as teaching aids, not so much for educating the 'heathen' about Europe but, in presenting these versions as great literature dealing in 'universals', for the purpose of inculcating in the mind of the colonial the natural rightness of his or her inferiority.

Olive Senior's poem, 'Colonial Girls School', in her 1985 collection (26–7) is often quoted in epigraphs to discussions of the female experience of such education: under the 'pale northern eyes', the sexuality, vitality, black skins, kinky hair and Creole language of West Indian girls was 'erased' until

> There was nothing left of ourselves.
> Nothing about us at all.

The fictional equivalent of Senior's poem must be *Crick Crack Monkey*. Now, it has been the custom to treat this text in terms of the 'double consciousness' of the protagonist Tee, torn between the secure and nurturing folk world of Tantie and the alienating, neo-colonial middle-class world of Auntie Beatrice (Thorpe, 1977; Paravisini and Webb, 1988: 108). These two female guardians come to represent conflicting class, colour and linguistic models for the child, as well as conflicting gender roles from which she must choose: the vocal, sensuous and independent Tantie versus Aunt Beatrice, 'Angel of the House' who wants to indoctrinate Tee into the 'ways of nice people' which means, for a girl, private school, dance lessons, tea parties, middle-class young men and so on.

However, Paravisini and Webb (109) have also pointed out that even in Tantie's realm, Tee faces the school system which is designed to teach allegiance to the British Empire and 'it is precisely [here] in *books* that she unconsciously learns her first lesson in duality and self-effacement.' Gikandi, approaching the novel from a different perspective, none the less supports the view that Tee belongs to all, and to none, of the communities she encounters (those of Tantie, Ma, Aunt Beatrice and the colonial school). The text does not, in his opinion, conform to Thorpe's suggestion of a movement from security to alienation, although such may be the adult narrator's retrospective nostalgic opinion. 'But', maintains Gikandi, 'from the perspective of Tee the child, there is a strong ambivalence toward oppositions such as alienation/security, Beatrice/Tantie; in none of these worlds can she posit herself as a subject.' (26)

No matter how 'at home' Tee feels in Tantie's world, he points out, she is aware of its marginalization and longs for the power that schooling will bring. And with schooling comes doubleness, self-estrangement, a loss of sense of self. For in school, Gikandi (27) explains, 'the tangible reality of the creole culture is dismissed as an unreal construct, while the fictions promoted by the colonial textbook are now adopted as the "real" Caribbean referent.' In Tee's words,

Books transported you always into the familiar solidity of chimneys and apple trees, the enviable normality of real Girls and Boys who went a-sleighing. . . . Books transported you always into Reality and Rightness, which were to be found Abroad. (*Crick Crack Monkey*, 61)

So begins Tee's apprehension of herself as inferior Other, to the imaginary white, English double that, for a time, she christens Helen. 'Helen' is the norm, Tee the Other, her subjectivity usurped. Helen is 'the proper ME', the *right* kind of girl – according to the books.

Such a process is termed 'spirit thievery' in Brodber's *Myal*, which also charts the internalization of the 'natural' relationship between European reality and native margin that gives rise to an alienation (in the colonized) of such severity as to be imaged as 'zombification'. As Brodber (1982) explains,

I have this notion that colonialism, as it operated in [the West Indies], was a theft of culture – a theft in a strange way. The English have brought in all these African peoples, who have a particular world view, and they insist on taking this world view away from them, which is in fact their *spirit*. Without it, you cannot live; without it you're just plain 'flesh' . . . only dry bones, rotten flesh.

Zombification ('flesh that takes directions from someone', *Myal* (108)) results from the trauma of being forcibly rewritten by imperial discourse, and then attempting the futile task of living as a subject in relation to one's scripted Otherness.

A society of zombies is, obviously, an unhealthy society. Appropriately, *Myal* examines such a society in microcosm through the mysterious swelling-sickness of Ella O'Grady Langley. Ella embodies the Jamaican national motto ('Out of Many, One People') as she does its history of plantation interculturation (she is mulatto, of Irish/Jamaican parentage, and married to an American). In the Afro-Jamaican peasant community of Grove Town she is an outsider, like the Revd William Brassington: 'One strange face in a sea of colour. Lonely among . . . [her] own people' (17). Compensating for her invisibility in her own world, she imaginatively enters the world of 'away' – maps of Europe, books of English Literature – and floats through her Grove Town life like a ghost, her mind, quite literally, elsewhere. Hence Maydene Brassington's impression of her as 'flying. Totally separated from the platform and from the people around her.' (17).

What Maydene also intuits is that this isolated, unrooted and ethereal existence is distressing to the child: 'she is not happy up there in the sky.

She wants to be real' (17). Attempting to mitigate Ella's ontological insecurity, the Brassingtons adopt her, pay for her training and allow her to travel as 'ladies companion' to the United States.

Here, she meets Selwyn Langley (ironically, as it turns out, the last in a long line of healers) who successfully courts her, marries her and proceeds to rewrite her. No African ancestry *please* – she is to say that *both* her parents were Irish; then comes 'the powdering and the plucking of eyebrows, the straightening of the hair, all of which a loving husband did. . . . The creator loved his creature' (43). Selwyn's task is easy, for Ella, like Tee, 'had a lifetime of practice' living in other people's fictions, and those whom he wishes Ella to approximate are similar to 'the pale-skinned people floating' in the texts she has learned by heart.

A true imperialist, Selwyn also appropriates Ella's past in the colonization of her body. For it is in the discovery of her sexuality that Ella experiences herself as 'real', connected at last to her remembered Jamaican world that comes alive under Selwyn's insistent probing. Having rewritten Ella, he withdraws, prematurely for Ella, who wants a future – a child – as well as her reconstructed past. His farewell gift is another authorial creation, a master-narrative of her history: an entertainment called 'Caribbean Nights and Days', 'the biggest coon show ever [staged]' (80).

Ella's horror at this travesty of her past, this 'spirit theft', in which she realises she has colluded, causes her to 'trip out'. She is silent, swells with a phantom pregnancy that no Western medicine can cure, and exhibits symptoms of 'the divided self' as discussed in Chapter 2; for example, she holds 'long conversations between her selves' (84). Ella's reintegration is as much a spiritual as a physical process. The myal man, Maas Cyrus (Percy the chick), who effects the cure is both natropath (healing with natural remedies) and 'restorer of spirits'.[1] In addition, he works with a 'healing team' that includes members of Ella's community: Baptist Minister Simpson (Mr Dan); dreadlocked hermit Ole African (Master Willie); Kumina church leader Miss Gatha (Mother Hen) and Maydene Brassington (White Hen), English wife of the Methodist pastor. As a group, they constitute a continuum of resources, from herbalism to religious, and thus educational, subversive potential. If 'spirit thievery comes in so many forms', it must be countered with all kinds of knowledge.

Ella's adoptive father lends his support, but this is a mutual affair. For in taking her to the myal man for help, the Reverend Brassington too 'was promised a cure' (94). In fact, it is in the figure of the mulatto William that Brodber's exposure of the imperial mission is most thorough. Like Ella, he is a victim of definition through European *pre-text*. However, his sense of his ministry coincides with Kipling's injunction (prettily recited by Ella early in the novel) to

Take up the whiteman's burden . . .
Go bind your sons to exile
To serve your captive's need . . . [that is:]
Your new caught sullen peoples
Half devil and half child (6).

William sees his community in terms of its representation in colonial discourse: 'My people have a far way to go and a far way we can go but we must understand how far back we are and submit so that we can learn' (21). His task, as he sees it, is to 'exorcise and replace' (18): exorcise traditional Afro-Jamaican practices and values and replace them with 'civilized' Western thinking and Christianity. No wonder his wife accuses him of 'taking away these people's spirit' (18).

The final section of the novel deals with the reconstruction of the colonial subject, the restoration of 'zombi' to full personhood, again through the educational system: 'Get in their books and know their truth, then turn around [slave] ship and books' (67). That is, expose and subvert the texts of empire: 'correct images from the inside, destroy what should be destroyed, replace it with what it should be replaced and put us back together' (110). The reverse of Willaim's exorcizing ministry, Ella's mission now is nothing short of rewriting the colonial subject!

Her job demands that she teach the 'parable' of Mr Joe's (Animal) farm in the *Caribbean Reader* familiar to generations of West Indians. The story tells of enslaved animals, alienated from their natural functions, who decide to rebel. Subsequently discovering in their 'freedom' that they are still utterly dependent, they meekly return to their masters, to a subordinate existence as 'living deads capable only of receiving orders from someone else and carrying them out' (107). Ella is repulsed by this reduction of individuals to 'sub-normals who have no hope of growth' (97) and worse, by her own role of inviting eager youngsters 'into complicity' in the (natural) truth that 'most of the world is made up of zombies who cannot think for themselves or take care of themselves but must be taken care of' (107). In discussion, the colonizing intentionality is exposed and *both* Ella and William decide to teach against the text by pointing out its bias, so telling '[t]he half [that] has never been told' (34).

Katrak (169) has noted that literary texts offer strategies for decolonizing culture. Here, Tiffin (1989b: 17) makes the crucial observation that *Myal* both *describes* 'counter-discursive strategy, which reads the social text of colonialist power and exposes and dismantles it', *and* is itself a paradigmatic theoretical document in demonstrating that '[t]extuality and politics are inseparable, complicit in the colonialist enterprise' (Tiffin, 1989a: 30). The novel shows the interrogation and unmasking of European 'pre-texts' to be crucial to the decolonization process.

Read from a post-colonial perspective, the novel's reinterpretation of the animal fable is a rewriting of colonial history as spirit thievery, and valorization of communal self-empowerment. Through the healing team (a truly hybrid group), Ella, the devalued female native, contextualizes herself as an agent, a subject where the imperial parable had only a passive 'half devil and half child'. A further dimension is added when we consider the issue of gender. Given that the practice of fiction is inevitably loaded, often related to an epistemology that justifies patriarchal and imperial assumptions, what difficulties are faced by the *female* Caribbean writer in constituting a *female* subject? For if the 'native' is primarily written as the site of European self-presence, the woman is that of the 'normal', universal subject: the male. She is necessary to the maintenance of his primacy because of her supposedly characteristic attributes (passivity, corporeality, emotional excess, irrationality, and so on) which 'prove' the male's superior 'difference' and justify her subjugation for her own, the children's, the society's sake. If selfhood, identity as subject, as a concept in patriarchal discourse, rests upon feminine alterity, then full subject-status is denied woman.

Feminist re-readings of the Euro-American canon have exposed this reasoning, but what of the West Indian canon? Until fairly recently, this was very much male-dominated,[2] and, as noted, representation of woman was generally consolidation of stereotype (self-sacrificing matriarch; inarticulate victim; sexual chattel; symbol of transcendent value) or relegation to the periphery of narrative.

For the Caribbean woman writer, then, the literary conception of subject/character (the norm of human-ness) has been male. Patricia Waugh's relevant study, *Feminine Fictions* seeks to account for the nature of subjectivity in patriarchal discourse by referring to psychoanalytic theory, particularly that of Jacques Lacan. For the male, she claims, much psychoanalytic theory seems to suggest that

> selfhood is conceived in terms of disidentification with the mother and identification with a father who symbolizes the larger culture, [and] it is the father who is seen to carry the reality principle. For a boy, the disidentification with the mother will be more radical and selfhood more likely to be defined absolutely in terms of autonomy and objective distance. (72)

Waugh concludes that men are psychologically and socially developed to exaggerate separateness and deny affective connection as the *basis* of identity (85). Their subjectivity involves splitting off the unbounded, the inchoate and the emotional on to women (who are associated with the earlier pre-oedipal period of non-separation from, and then total dependency on, the mother figure).

However, Lacan views *all* human agency, determination and identity as merely the illusory effects of the individual's positioning within a (patriarchal) 'Symbolic Order' which necessarily *pre-exists* him or her. Lacanian thinking thus supports postmodernist literary theory's discrediting of the 'unitary, self-directing, isolated ego' as subject. The matrix of textuality renders invalid the conventional novelistic subject/character. Similarly, since the text is an interplay of infinite possibilities of signification, my concern with the intentions of the female writer becomes irrelevant; it is the reader who is the site of meaning, for the text is an *event* which happens to, and only with the participation of, the reader.

But Waugh raises a crucial point when she notes that

> for those marginalized by the dominant culture, a sense of identity as constructed through impersonal and social relations of power (rather than a sense of identity as the reflection of an inner 'essence') has been a major aspect of their self-concept long before post-structuralists and post-modernists began to assemble their cultural manifestos (3).

Postmodernism, she feels, stresses the inability of the contemporary subject to locate 'himself' historically; feminist theory, however, starts from the *necessity* of locating the female subject: that is, 'a sense of effective agency and history for women which has hitherto been denied them by the dominant culture' (9). Helen Tiffin too has queried 'post-structuralism's critique of the centred subject' because she feels it has often 'displaced a historically specific, culturally grounded critique of colonialist power and subsumed real social difference in a Western obsession with epistemological legitimation' (1989b: 7). The postmodernist position on subjectivity, then, may not be that of the feminist or post-colonial writer.[3] Certainly Hutcheon's defence of the usefulness of postmodernist thought to post-colonial criticism (for example, its questioning of all totalizing systems, and its dialogue with history) still concedes that

> current post-structuralist/post-modern challenges to the coherent, autonomous subject have to be put on hold in feminist and post-colonial discourses, for both must work first to assert and affirm a denied or alienated subjectivity. (151)

At the same time, as Dash (17–18) has pointed out, the whole notion of self-formation or 'subjectification' has preoccupied Caribbean writers long before it became 'a major philosophical issue in post-modernist thought' (19). In different Caribbean texts he sees represented a 'self-certain subject, free to confer meaning on his or her world, to wrest the land from Prospero's signifying grasp' *and* a deconstruction of such a 'sovereign subject', who is represented rather as the site 'where collective subject finds articulation, where private and public, individual and group interact' (18–19). The questioning of the 'sovereign subject' then, is part of the Caribbean literary tradition as a whole, and regional women's writing too has, as Balutansky (forthcoming, 13–14) points out, critiqued imperialistic individualism. She cites Spivak in arguing that such 'individualism' is no better in the female than in the male, distinguishing a female 'individualist' from a female individual who asserts her agency without reinscribing imperialistic impulses.

We may conclude then, that the necessity for locating a coherent female subject *is* important in West Indian women's writing but, at the same time, that texts reflect unease with the male norm of 'unitary, self-directing, isolated ego' which postmodernism has thrown out or, more accurately suspended. Waugh concedes that some women writers – she does not confine herself to any geographic location – accept the inevitable alienation of the female 'I' in patriarchal discourse, and feature in their fictions 'mad' schizophrenic or paranoic women who experience themselves as culturally defined *images* – and thus, in effect, as nothing – as explored in Chapter 2.

But what, she asks (10) if we conceive of a different kind of subject, such as 'a collective concept of subjectivity which foregrounds the construction of identity *in relationship*'? Rather than seeing the self come into being at the moment of radical disidentification with the mother/Other – who then becomes that against which the individual *defines* his or her subjectivity, Waugh looks to Nancy Chodorow's notion of the infant as object-seeking (as against Freud's pleasure-seeking), which suggests that its basic desire is for relationship. Weedon (58–9) explains Chodorow's thesis that mother/daughter bonding is stronger than that between mother and son, resulting in a lesser degree of individuation in girls who, as a result, develop 'more flexible ego boundaries'; men tend to lack the extended personal relations women maintain, and base their relationships less on affective ties than 'on abstract, universalistic role expectations'. Laura Abruna (1990: 89) also discusses Chodorow's concept of women's relational development, and its extension in the work of Carol Gilligan, who sees masculinity as defined 'through separation, individuation, and achievement, whereas femininity is defined through intimacy, relationships with other people, and an ethnic of caring.' While identity is seen within patriarchy as valuing autonomy over reciprocity, Abruna considers that Caribbean women writers privilege relational interaction in their texts (90), and gives several examples, particularly of female bonding.

Waugh's scope is broader. She cites writers such as Doris Lessing, Margaret Atwood, Toni Morrison and Alice Walker as refusing in their fictions any unitary concept of self that needs Other as self-evident opposite, and seeming less interested in the quest of the isolated individual than in positing a character who recognizes her construction (from a range of subject positions available in several discourses) through the collective. Instead of division from, mutuality with. So, while acknowledging that there is no *one* female style, she observes that '[i]n formal aesthetic terms, breaking down boundaries, loosening distinct outlines, merging the individual with the collective, and exploring the ambiguity of identity at the interface of subject and object are likely to be stronger in women writers' (80–81). Narrative strategy thus facilitates a vision of society

> where, indeed, difference would not be separation, but connection which does not threaten autonomy – a collectivism that preserves the individual self. Such writing constructs a new subject, one who is necessarily 'dispersed' but who is also an effective agent, neither the old liberal subject nor the contemporary post-structuralist site of the play of signification (169).

The relevance of Waugh's alternative textual construction of female subjectivity ('in relationship' 'through the collective') to Brodber's *Myal* is striking.[4] Chapter 3 points to the reconstruction of Nellie, in *Jane and Louisa Will Soon Come Home*, as involving what Joyce Walker Johnson (55) calls a 'repairing of the breach' – between economic, racial and gender groups, between generations – within her community/her self. In *Myal*, the construction of Ella, the female subject, initially involves 'domination by consent' at the hands of the male author, Selwyn. She is entirely dependent ('hooked') on his directions and ministrations. Ultimately, Ella is his creature, empty of herself and forbidden to do/make anything (including a child) within the relationship. Like Antoinette, she becomes a shadowy Other to her husband, a zombi, a 'marvellously sculpted work waiting for the animator' (*Myal*: 46). A subplot in the novel concerns another instance of spirit thievery, in Maas Levi's attempt to restore his potency (his maleness, his self-presence) at the expense of female subjectivity (Anita's spirit) by misuse of ancestral obeah ritual.

Having demonstrated the way in which patriarchy appropriates female subjectivity, how does the West Indian woman writer, here Erna Brodber, suggest an alternative? Waugh's insights are valuable in this context, for one can see Brodber affecting a reconstruction, an engineering of her female character/subject (as integrated agent rather than alienated zombi) by the collectivity of her society. The strategy is implicit in the text's narrative eclecticism.

Elsewhere (1990: 51) I have noted the elusive nature of narrative voice in *Myal*. The text demonstrates a 'diffusion' of the omniscient narrator's power of representation through employment of what Helen Tiffin has termed an 'alter/native' mode of telling that must, because it draws on the oral creole tradition (and the social history encoded therein) be communal.

So *many* voices input into the telling: 'Everybody thought. . . . Miss Iris did
not know. . . . Things started from early. . . . Cook say it was like. . . .' In
so far as one can occasionally identify an authorial voice, it speaks the
language of the community (living and dead) and moves fluidly from ironic
detachment to intimate in-group 'susu':

> As is usual, this new officer came to town with no wife and needed a
> housekeeper. As is also usual, the housekeeper was before long in the
> family way. What was unusual, was for said housekeeper to refuse to
> move to Kingston's anonymity to be kept by her baby-father and to
> opt to go back to her country bush. . . . so although he did have every
> desire to do right by Mary, things had to finish, done, end: they had
> was to part, my dear. (6)

In addition, this communal voice employs a wide range of discursive
techniques: for example, the early discussion of Ella's origins (6–9) utilizes
religious, scientific, myalist, folkloric explanations, as well as salacious
gossip. Narrative 'voice' may take on the tone of newscaster (3–4); porten-
tous introduction ('The words were the words of Kipling but the voice was
that of Ella O'Grady aged 13' (5)); wry humourist ('the next item on the
programme . . .' (71)); or punster ('there was no mutiny on that bounty
though' (101)). Readers are treated to anecdotes, songs and spells, statistics,
dreams and lyrical fantasies, cosy practical wisdom, schoolbook stories and
parables, and the local frame of reference undoubtedly loses some non-
Jamaicans. The overall effect becomes less a medley of voices than a
collective voice with its own internal logic and contradictions.

Furthermore, Ella's healing (bringing into being as a subject) is the
collective effort of a powerful group within Grove Town society. They are
from different nationalities, races, sexes and backgrounds; they transcend
spatial boundaries, communicating via a kind of telepathy; they cross boundaries of time, in that the group comprises individual characters who *also*
embody elements of ancestral personalities; they even transcend genre
distinctions: each of these characters in Brodber's story is also a character
in the schoolbook allegory of Mr Joe's farm. Both distinct personalities *and*
a composite force, simultaneously represented in two different but related
texts, part of the Grove Town moment and incarnate ancestral presences,
they function like separate instruments whose meaning/power exists in the
fusion of musical performance.

Following Brathwaite's classical analysis of Roger Mais's *Brother
Man* as 'jazz novel', one notes the importance of musical terminology,
particularly in connection with the healing team, from the first page of
Myal. For example, their dialogue is a kind of scribal equivalent of a 'jam
session': the references to playing together, to drum, trumpet and cymbal
(38); the vocabulary of 'yeah, yeah . . . no one hits those notes better than

you' (39); the rapid to-and-fro of call and response, of reiterated refrain (66–7); the soaring, improvised solo (99) and duet (110–11) give new meaning to my notion of the author as 'sound engineer' of the dub version! If sound, music stands for an alter/native discourse (and epistemology) then the accusation of those who 'stole our sound' (66) is yet another reference to spirit thievery.

My point is that the group works by negotiating different 'realities' (Myalism, Kumina, West Indian variants of the Baptist and Methodist faith) as well as different, hybrid discourses, to those of the 'spirit thieves'. The fractured, 'pre-scripted' history of the colonial subject is recuperated and revalidated within the group's own, diffuse creole articulation that is outside the comprehension and control of the 'master narrative'.

One could argue, with Waugh, that *Myal* illustrates a certain 'female style': Brodber's narrative transcends boundaries between reality and illusion, loosens distinct outlines of characters (living and dead, fictional and 'metafictional') and merges individual with collective personality in an exploration of the ambiguity of identity. Her dispensing with a single authoritative voice is a feature common to other Caribbean women writers: Suzanne Crosta observes of Maryse Condé's latest novel, *Traversée de la Mangrove* (1989) that at the narrative centre of the work is not a single vision, but rather a kind of 'multiple individual' whose divergent perspectives resist any specific representation of reality. Daryl Dance (1990), in her discussion of texts by Caribbean and Afro-American women that treat of female characters in a state of fragmentation, notes that they share a process 'of psychic healing that grows out of a community . . . and moves each character towards . . . a reclaiming of self within the black community' (182), suggesting a common focus on 'relational subjectivity' also.

On the other hand, since Brodber clearly eschews any notion of fixed, unitary subject in this novel which details such various modes of being, and utilizes formal techniques that challenge genre distinction and conventions of realism that self-consciously play with fictional expectations – techniques Hutcheon (151) identifies as postmodernist – one could argue that her work can be located within post-structuralist practice. Such practice emphasizes meaning as constituted within language (within particular, sometimes conflicting, discursive fields each of which offer certain subject positions) so that any subjectivity posited is unstable, changing, or as Chris Weedon puts it, always 'in process'. *Myal* would seem to fit this bill.

Indeed, Gikandi considers that while many West Indian women writers may not be sympathetic to certain aspects of postmodernism, yet 'they increasingly fall back on post-modernist narrative strategies – such as temporal fragmentation, intertextuality, parody and doubling – to devalorize the modernist project' (19). However, to complicate matters, Helen Tiffin (1988) maintains that a number of literary strategies – refusal of closure, a move away from realist representation, the interrogation of binary structuration – 'are characteristic of both the generally post-colonial and the European post-modern' (172); *although* she notes that such strategies are energised by quite different theoretical assumptions and political motivations. Formal experiments in literary fragmentation can, for example, be traced to indigenous ontology and epistemology, as she demonstrates in her analysis of Chinua Achebe's *Things Fall Apart* (174–5), while in Caribbean post-colonial fictions, the interrogation of history and textuality informs the frequent thematization of escape from the constraints of written records (176).

In the end, these various theoretical orientations offer points of overlap that can only be useful to the 'woman version' of West Indian literature. The main criterion for critical appropriation remains, for me, political efficacy. Brodber's *Myal* does not suspend the notion of an integrated, historically located female subject even as it demonstrates that identity is a communal affair, impossible of achievement in defensive isolation *or* at the expense of devalued Other. In that Brodber's collective narrative (literally) 'author/izes' the reconstructed Ella, her maturity as a subject (Waugh's term) comes through her recognition of the relational nature of her identity and her commitment to the preservation of her community's 'spirit' at the end of the novel.

Yes, one can accept that the subject, female as male, is 'historically determined and discursively oriented' (Waugh, 210); but *Myal* also demonstrates Waugh's contention that 'human will, subversive desire, and the consolidation of human connectedness can still exist as effective forces of political change.' It is fitting that what Mordecai and Wilson (xiv) call 'the problem of the restoration of community in the West Indies' receives committed attention by a West Indian woman writer like Brodber, through her fictional engineering of the female subject.

Notes

1   See Nadine Wilkins (28) on the physical and metaphysical nature of myalism.
2   See Mordecai and Wilson (ix–x).
3   Chris Weedon, however, tries to reconcile post-structuralist discourse theory and feminist practice, arguing (125) that while post-structuralism does 'deny the authenticity of individual experience by decentring the national unitary, autonomous subject of literary humanism, or the essential female nature at the centre of much radical feminism, rendering it socially constituted within discourse' the female individual none the less 'exists as a thinking, feeling subject and social agent, capable of resistance and innovations produced out of the clash between contradictory subject positions and practices . . . and able to choose from the options available.'
4   See also Ashcroft (33) on the 'plural process' of woman's being, due to the pre-oedipal mother-daughter relationship.

CHAPTER 5 | A 'carnival' set-up

Ironic/double reading

In the previous chapters, I have argued that West Indian women's fictions, taken together, evade dogmatic theoretical del:neations as to *who* may speak about *what* in *which* voice or language. In fact, the 'woman version' is quite irreverent in choice of subject position, narrative strategy and relations with any 'original cut' or master narrative. I have also focused on ways in which some of the fictions demonstrate a feminist and post-colonial desire to avoid inscription strictly in oppositional terms. As Ashcroft, Griffiths and Tiffin acknowledge (169–70), subjects *are* inevitably interpellated within ideologies, but to choose simply to react – for example, by being a 'Bad' subject within imperial discourse – 'may inadvertently support what it seeks to oppose by confirming a "symmetry" between the two' (170). In feminist thinking we can perceive a similar desire to avoid 'counter determination' in, say Hélène Cixous's abhorrence of terms like 'masculine' and 'feminine' which imprison us within the binary logic of patriarchy.

Given certain similarities of strategy and political outlook, theoretical cross-fertilization of the kind recommended by Ashcroft (1989) can be helpful in reading texts by West Indian women. An example is Hutcheon's observation (154) that post-colonial *and* postmodernist writing share a strategic concern with

> the use of the trope of irony as a doubled or split discourse which has the potential to subvert from within. . . .[:] as a double-talking, forked-tongued mode of address, irony becomes a popular rhetorical strategy for working within existing discourses and contesting them at the same time.

Such 'doubleness' – of vision, of narrative perspective, of language – is central to the situation of the West Indian woman, doubly colonized, and is reflected in texts that articulate her experience.

An initial reading of Grace Nichols's *Whole of a Morning Sky* suggests that double or ironic vision informs the organization of the narrative. The novel is a thinly-fictionalized memoir of Guyanese social history between the early 1950s and the mid-1960s. Most of the text is taken up with the arrival of the Walcott family in Georgetown in the election year of 1960, their integration into urban society and the *dis*integration of the city due to political and racial tribalism. Episodically, Nichols details the arson which decimated Georgetown; the general strikes and violence which crippled the economy and brought down Cheddi Jagan's popularly elected People's Progressive Party (the NLP of the novel); and the Anglo-American role in this destabilization, which resulted in the ascendancy of Forbes Burnham's party. The nominally central consciousness is that of the child Gem; as in Edgell's *Beka Lamb* and Shinebourne's *Timepiece*, her development is linked to that of her young and struggling nation. Accordingly, *Whole of a Morning Sky* can be said to share in the nationalist project of rewriting history that has been very much a part of the West Indian literary tradition.

The first of the novel's prefatory epigraphs reads as follows:

> were some who ran one way.
> were some who ran another way.
> were some who did not run at all.
> were some who will not run again.
> And I was with them all,
> when the sun and streets exploded,
> and a city of clerks
> turned a city of men!
> was a day that had to come,
> ever since the whole of a morning sky,
> glowed red like glory,
> over the tops of houses.

The piece is credited to fellow-Guyanese, Martin Carter, but the title of the poem is omitted. Accordingly, one is free to respond to the extract rather than the entire composition (which is, of course, 'Good Friday, 1962' and conveys in its totality a *quite* different impression to that teased out in Nichols's text). Here, the lines suggest apocalypse, but in a positive sense: violent social change as a glorious upheaval. A chaotic, fragmented society, running in all directions, explodes into a revolution that transforms emasculated 'clerks' into heroic 'men' (and the odd martyr/casualty who 'will not run again'). The process is seen, in retrospect, as inevitable, just and right, thus elevated to 'glory'.

The prose narrative which follows can be read as an ironic counterpoint to the extract (*not* the whole poem), demonstrating the incongruity of its embedded sentiments. Filtered through the consciousness of the power-less (mostly women) who are caught 'in the crossfire', violent political upheaval – whether state-sanctioned war or popularly-sanctioned revolution – emerges as inimical to human life, and unjustified *whatever* its ideological motivation. The 'clerks' turned 'men', the heroic soldiers of the cause, are deflated, emerging as pathetic puppets controlled by external hegemonic interests who exploit racial and political faction.

Whole of a Morning Sky picks up key motifs in the excerpt and subverts their emotional appeal by re-contextualization. The novel's opening lines read: 'You run fast alongside the red brick public road' (1); but unlike the directionless, divided mob of the extract, the girl-child here is certain in her trajectory and her purpose: laying claim to her own 'piece of earth' (the village and backdam) which she shares with an integrated, multiracial community.

The Walcotts are leaving this rural Eden because the retired patriarch wishes his children to share in the progress and modernity of the capital, the 'city of clerks'. Her flight suggests a desire to evade this vision of her future, which as the extract forewarns, will be quite different from the father's conception; thus, her running through the village culminates, not in awareness of optimism and future glory, but in images of blood, pain and 'a haze of tears' (3).

In fact, the narrative itself mimics Gem's flight along different paths: it explores different racial and political orientations, different consciousnesses, different 'subject positions', achieving 'polyphonic' richness despite its geographical and temporal specificity. Disjointed or fluid movement compares positively, as narrative methodology, with the fragmentation of the extract's opening lines. A 'double' vision enables the reader to see and evaluate both patterns, and the 'open consciousness' of the child is a device for accommodating a variety of personal and political opinions and 'truths'.[1] One recalls the epigraph's omniscient stance: 'And I was with them all'.

Despite the exploration of different paths, we are aware early on of an inexorability of events similarly evoked in the extract ('was a day that had to come'). However, the tone of righteous anticipation in the poem is undercut in the text. In the natural and human realm, signs and portents ('Clara's big brown and white cat gave birth to three kittens, and devoured them almost immediately' (37)) prefigure doom rather than glory. Malevolent powers – British and American (70) – are waiting in the wings.

Part Two of the novel anatomizes the 'city of clerks', both literally (Gem's sister works in the Civil Service, her department consisting of lazy, opinionated but powerless drones) and figuratively. Divisions within institutions indicated in the first four lines of the extract, along political and racial lines, are shown to be largely a matter of fabrication. The reputedly government-controlled, pro-Indian Civil Service is anything but. Deft exposure of lies, prejudices and half-truths casts the revolutionary indignation of the extract in an ironic light: it is rhetoric rather than reality which fuels the crisis, and those who live it are muddled and confused by the various calls to action.

The glorification of infuriate purgation in the last three lines of the epigraph is, again, ironically undercut in the extended use of fire imagery in Nichols's narrative. The canefields in which Indian sugar workers toil are described as infernos (81); news of the strike by the exploited black labour force is 'carried through the streets . . . like windblown bits of burnt cane leaves' (81). The Guyanese working class – for all their acquiescence in the racial 'divide-and-rule' ploy of the unscrupulous – are united in this imagery: they will be the victims of the fire.

Similarly, the 'exploding sun' of the extract, suggesting cosmic concurrence with social revolution, translates in the narrative into a pitiless oppressor 'beating down on the mass demonstration' (97). What comes is no glorious purge, but a scorching waste, a debilitating excess of violent force, and the city on fire is compared to a 'biblical catastrophe' (105). All that remains, counter to the 'city of men' triumphant in the epigraph, is twisted black wreckage and huddled, 'chastened little crowds' (111) in awe of the foreign troops who have assumed control of Guyana's destiny.

The flames of racial hatred remain unabated, culminating in the deliberate atrocity of Gem's little friend, 'Teddy and all his seven brothers and sisters burning to death' before her eyes (149). Gem asks for reasons for the murder. 'You wouldn't understand', replies her mother, 'It's political' (149). The mood of political fervour in the extract is effectively shattered in the parallel narrative, where 'politics' is seen as death-dealing and futile. One is reminded of Wilfred Owen's strategy in '*Dulce et decorum est*'; and of course, this is the point of Carter's (1977) poem, taken in its full context. The poem concludes

> True, was with them all,
> and told them more than once:
> in despair there is hope, but there is none in death.
> Now I repeat it here, feeling a waste of life,
> In a market-place of doom, watching the human face!

The poem *in its entirety* is 'a telling repudiation' of the horrors chronicled in the novel; the sentiments isolated *in the epigraph* are exposed as condoning such horrors. As such, the novel serves as a 'woman version' that signifies against any political philosophy in the West Indies which valorizes violent confrontation as the only true means to social liberation.

Carnivalesque comic vision

The exposure of political violence in Nichols's narrative ironization of the epigraph leads into a different type of exposure in *Whole of a Morning Sky*, one central to what has been called 'comic vision'. One familiar type of comic vision utilizes laughter to reduce the target, suggesting a lack of connection between mocking observer and humiliated object, or else an uneasy denial of that link. Laughter is aggressive; the joke is at someone's expense, and the aim is punitive revelation for the ostensible restoration of proper behaviour.

On the other hand, there is comic vision which entails subversion, which defies or challenges the codes of rational, hierarchical 'anticomic' society in order to effect a transformation, usually dramatized in reunions, reconciliations and communal celebration. Laughter here is irreverent but also sympathetic; the targets are often pretension, hypocrisy, and unjust tyranny.

I would suggest that it is this latter type of 'comic vision' that surfaces in some West Indian women's writing: in parts of *Crick Crack Monkey*, *Beka Lamb*, the fiction of Erna Brodber and several of Olive Senior's stories. Indeed, Esteves and Paravisini-Gebert (xvii) suggest that Caribbean women's fiction in general reveals irreverently subversive impulses, particularly targeting middle-class, patriarchal notions of respectability and 'normal behaviour' in the realm of gender roles. Patricia Waugh's observation (93) on Virginia Woolf's use of comedy maps out the territory I wish to explore: that which undermines 'the edifices of the "masculine" intelligence (its rituals, titles, buildings, limousines, legal, medical, and educational institutions), which reify the system at the expense of the human beings it is intended to serve.' Women's writing, then, exposes – sometimes humorously – as a means of decentring patriarchal discourse by uncovering the fallacy of privilege *necessarily* accruing to certain forms of behaviour, certain institutions and values.

Bakhtin's ideas on parody and the 'carnivalesque' narrative are particularly useful in this context. Bakhtin traces parodic-travestying literature back to the folk humour of Europe in classical times, and particularly during the Medieval and Renaissance eras, when carnival festivities provided a 'boundless world of humorous forms and manifestations [which] opposed the official and serious tone of medieval ecclesiastical and feudal culture' (1984: 4). While official Church feasts asserted the existing order, carnival festivals temporarily liberated people 'from the prevailing truth and from the established order; it marked the suspension of all hierarchical rank, privileges, norms, and prohibitions' (1984: 10). The carnival was a time of becoming, change, renewal, allowing interaction according to 'new, purely human relations' (10).

The logic of carnival is that of parody, of deconstructive comic inversion, turning everything inside out; rather different from the 'negative and formal parody' of modern times (11): 'The present-day analysis of laughter explains it either as purely negative satire . . . or else as gay, fanciful, recreational drollery deprived of philosophic content' (12). Carnival laughter is far more complex in nature: it is gay, liberating and regenerative in impulse, and takes place in a communal context; it is ambivalent (can be triumphant and mocking); it is directed at the entire world, including those who laugh.

Parodic carnival literature then, introduces the 'permanent corrective of laughter . . . the corrective of reality that is always richer, more fundamental and most importantly *too contradictory and heteroglot* to be fitted into a high and straightforward genre' (1988: 136). Parody, like irony (to which it is of course related) is, to recall Hutcheon's point at the start of this chapter, ' doubled or split discourse which has the potential to subvert from within.' The comic vision can be subversive of the established hierarchies, and – at least temporarily – transformative of the old relations and differences.

So, of course, can another kind of writing: *écriture féminine*, Cixous's 'feminine writing'. As noted at the start of this chapter, Cixous's wish to undermine the binary oppositionals, masculine/feminine, lead her to postulate a new 'bisexuality' in which either sex can write in a masculine or a feminine way. 'Feminine writing' isn't simply a woman's style of writing, but writing which relates to hegemonic power in a certain way: it rejects, or lacks, the masculine position *vis-à-vis* authority; it struggles to undermine dominant phallagocentric logic (Moi, 1991: 108). 'Feminine writing' then, as a concept resembles parodic carnival writing in seeking to deconstruct 'normal' hierarchies, undermining all authority, revelling in the carnival and the open-ended. As noted in Chapter 3, and as Moi (1991: 140) observes of another of the 'French feminist' theoreticians, Luce Irigaray, women cannot write in some pure realm outside of patriarchy. But they *can* utilize strategies which subvert from within; so Irigaray recommends parody, the mimicry of patriarchal discourse which by *over*doing it, *un*does it.

As well as political efficacy, a certain playful irreverence is common to these varying theoretical concepts, which I want to appropriate for this discussion of an impulse to 'comic vision' in some Caribbean women's texts. For instance, Olive Senior's popular story, in her 1986 collection, 'Do Angels wear Brassières?' demonstrates the subversive power of parody as Beccka mimics the sacred language of the Bible and the authoritarian catechism-interrogation of religious instruction to undermine 'righteous' adult authority, particularly that of Aunty Mary and Archdeacon:

By now Beccka and the Archdeacon exchanging Bible knowledge.
Beccka asking him question and he trying his best to answer but they
never really tell him any of these things in theological college
. . . .
'Who is the shortest man in the Bible?' Archdeacon groan.
'Peter. Because him sleep on his watch. Ha Ha Ha.'
'Ho Ho Ho Ho Ho.' (73–4).

Here, the normal hierarchical relations are inverted, sacred wisdom becomes comic and the girl-child triumphs over the powerful adult male.

To take another (not necessarily humorous) example, Ineke Phaf
(359) analyzes Astrid Roemer's *Life Long Poem* partly in terms of a
'carnivalization' of popular nation dogma: for Phaf, Roemer's 'nation-
perspective' subverts official nationalism, depicting 'nation reality' rather
as 'a changing and changeable process'. Post-colonial literatures do evince
a concern with developing definitions of national history but, as Esteves
and Paravisini-Gebert (xvi) point out of the Caribbean 'canon', the nationalist impulse often 'led to the neglect and devaluation of women's
writing, as the themes acceptable within the context of national formation
. . . often fell outside the boundaries of women's socio-historic experience.' However, Boehmer (10) considers that women writers have more
recently engaged with patriarchal nationalist texts and, as in the case of
Flora Nwapa, disrupted and/or transformed them by 'interrupting the
language of official nationalist discourse and literature with a women's
vocality.'

I want now to return to *Whole of a Morning Sky* and apply the general
notion of a parodic, subversive strategy to Nichols's interrogation of her
national history as firmly within patriarchal conventions.

In *Whole of a Morning Sky* political power and leadership are solidly
patriarchal. Those who lead the state, the political parties, the schools,
churches, and families are men. Nichols's narrative undermines their
phallogocentric (or, in Eagleton's wonderful phrase (189), 'cocksure') authority by a parodic send-up of their inflated rhetoric and by exposing their
manipulative self-interest as it impacts negatively on the day-to-day life of
the community, particularly in the domestic sphere. To put it simplistically,
the novel is an exercise in 'cutting down to size' via a female/comic vision
which privileges the preservation and celebration of life.

But Nichols's comic exposure is usually sympathetic: it laughs at
how seriously people take themselves and their problems. Male authority
figures, it transpires, share a common human frailty. What is risible is the
discovery of their masking this frailty behind pompous affectation or ideological rhetoric. So Archie Walcott, Gem's father, attempts to impress his
importance and seriousness of purpose upon his staff at the Highdam

School, but his rhetorical effect is undercut by unimpressed female body language:

> He spoke long and earnestly. He let it be known he would stand no nonsense. He was amazed at the teachers' habit of slipping in and out of school. He believed in a full day's work for a full day's pay. Teacher Mary . . . listened to all his new plans and instructions in an ominous silence, arms folded, nostrils flared. . . . (7)

In this description, the physical presence of Teacher Mary is a silent but powerful counterforce to Archie's clichés of authority.

Archie is conservative, politically and economically; in fact, he is mean (87). He insists on rank, proper names, a healthy and ordered regime, living by little rituals. Affecting the patriarch, he is a prime target for deflation: 'Gem, watching her father slowly chewing his food – Archie was always stressing the importance of chewing food – suddenly burst out laughing at the table, sending little bits of wet bread flying' (88). The womenfolk in his family gently mock his pettiness, pomposity and meanness, as does Nichols's narrative. For example, Archie fears communism as a threat to his hard-earned savings (23). Ironically, it is at a motorcade of the socialist premier that he *is* robbed – of 'his bicycle key, ball-point pen and a couple of coins' (55)!

But mockery of his rigidity and parsimony is always mediated by sympathy. His crippling worry about poverty has made him mean (85); his insecurity has made him class-conscious (18); his early loss of his parents has made him wary of emotion (17). Compassion is intrinsic to Nichols's comic vision. Even Dinah's bullying boss is humanized by the mention of his 'intolerable' position in the political structure (77).

Even where the narrative approaches satire at the expense of male political posturing, the exposure of chicanery is rarely vicious. Archie's cousin Lionel, for example, is one of the many opportunists who assemble a party and a manifesto to capitalize on the fervour for political democracy. This is only the latest of his ventures in pursuit of El Dorado and Nichols parodies the male 'conquistador' mind-set by describing his previous abortive adventures in pork-knocking ('he returned to the city two months later with severe bat bites and stories of how the other pork-knockers had tried to drown him' (31)) and making soap (with disastrous results for Clara's pots).

His apprenticeship in bravado, blurring the facts (to save face on his return from pork-knocking) and soft-soaping (he persuades Clara he knows what he is doing) serve him admirably on his entry into politics, as the empty clichés of his manifesto illustrate: 'Basically about self-government and a better way of life for the people. . . . But we wouldn't go for independence in a hurry' (33). The extent of his sincerity soon becomes apparent when he quits politics at the first setback.

My point is that this parody-travesty, exposing as it does the superficiality of political commitment and the depth of the politician's self-interest, utilizes an easy, anecdotal tone which precludes malice. The same good humour is maintained in the unmasking of other types of male political posturing: Atwell/Burnham's crowd-pleasing rhetoric; Dinah's pal Hartly, a revolutionary with his 'small haversack full of books by Marx and Engels' (61) who is also a snob and a misfit engaged in empty gestures of childish defiance (64). But the grim subtext of the novel, the horrific consequences of such pompous play-acting, mediate the irreverence with which such comic figures are 'set up.'

Power, employed in the humiliation and dehumanization of others, is antithetical to the transformative and humane impulses of comic vision. Again, it is through women's voices that authority figures – like the policeman who tries to shame those to whom he should be answerable (54) – are brought low. So the elderly 'small-chested' cousin delegated to drive the bride to church, who imperiously demands to know why she is late, is out of step with the carnival festivity and is taken down a peg or two by a neighbouring woman: 'But look de dry up old shrimp' (114). Economic tyranny is translated by an anti-communist woman into sexual appropriation: '"dem cammanists does take away everything. Down to yuh own quarter pound here," she said, putting her hand protectively between her legs, "yuh can't call yuh own" (97).' Again, the female body confronts abstract ideology.

In Olive Senior's work it is often the child who exposes the adult; here too, humour results from the exposure of adult authority as masking cruelty or depravity, as in the joke played on Chin the shopkeeper (49–50). In another episode, adult 'respectability' proves to be a thin veneer and Gem's parody of polite deference to the hungover old man she salutes repeatedly – 'Good morning, Master Castello' (*Master* Castello is over sixty) – is eventually greeted with something quite different than the courteous response demanded by convention:

> He would rise up slowly, his head shaking as if he were about to have a fit: 'Good morning, scunt! Good morning, rass!' he'd scream. 'Why de rass you don't tell yuh mother rass good morning?' (44)

Comedy here results from an inversion of the rules of polite exchange, from an incongruous loss of control and of course, from the Creole obscenity. While the deflationary use of the vernacular is not peculiar to West Indian women writers, Nichols exploits it to the full. Note, for example, linguistic shifts in the following passage, where incongruous juxtaposition of formal Biblical exhortation and earthy pronunciation operates similarly to Merle Hodge's wonderful phrase 'Them that walketh in the paths of corruption will live to ketch dey arse' (Mordecai and Wilson, 198). Note also, in this incident, Archie's reaction to his wife's comic sense:

> The preacher, a short stocky red man, kept on imploring them not to be caterpillars but to be butterflies. 'Let us nat be content with the life of sin and darkness, my friends. Let us strive towards de higha life. Let us not be content to be kyattapillas. Don't be a kyattapilla, my friends. I say be a buttafly,' he screamed.
>
> Archie had resigned himself to [Clara's] laughter, treating it the way one would treat the sudden giggling fit of a small child. . . . (8–9).

Clearly, it is the (childish?) female comic vision that sees the humorous clash here between the intention and the effect of the preacher's words.

Carolyn Cooper's recent (1992) study of *Annie John* notes the connection between patriarchal and imperial tyranny in the text: Annie's grandfather/Christopher Columbus/ the domineering Mineu who would always play master to Annie's servant, are conflated and then 'brought low'. Kincaid's text undercuts pompous patriarchy by narratively undermining what Cooper terms 'the blustering power of mini Columbuses' (9). Further, Cooper maintains that empathy with the vanquished villain on Annie's part allows for a reconfiguration of simple binary equations of identity (innocent native/demonic explorer) (11). In West Indian women's writing, dramatic irony, parodic deconstruction, a sympathetic comic vision that exposes without destroying, are some of the methods by which attempts on the part of patriarchal discourse to 'fix' roles as normative, are evaded. Nichols's text, like Kincaid's allusion to (and mockery of) the maps according to which woman/native is plotted, evinces a 'carnivalesque' wit and subtly opens up space for a more complex vision of human existence.

Communality, corporeality and domesticity

Bakhtin's notion of the 'carnivalesque' tradition is essentially communal, rooted in – but in literature not exclusive to – the folk tradition. In the previous chapter, I also argued that West Indian women's fiction tends to be communal in focus; and, of course, a celebration of community is central to the comic vision. In *Whole of a Morning Sky*, such an integrative pull is the province of women. By contrast with her mother, Gem's father is alienated from all but a select few of his countrymen. He despairs of city blacks (120), admires but distrusts Indians: '[h]e didn't trust anyone completely' (23). Aloof in his dignity, Archie tries to discourage his wife's familiarity with neighbours in Highdam (10) and in Georgetown (46).

Clara, on the other hand, suggests a communally oriented vision which can overcome racial and political, gender and class division; like her daughter, her wish is that Guyanese people will 'pull together' (80). Accordingly, she is represented as sympathetic to all, refusing boundaries of race and rank, and finds a great deal of support from other women whose 'gales of kitchen laughter' unsettle and provoke her husband (24); he feels 'on the edge of all this womanness' (10). This 'womanness' does not preclude female hostility (26, 44) nor does it romanticize woman as always 'caring': Miss Sheila supposedly threw acid on her lover (42) and Ivy Payne beats her children unmercifully (46). But the dominant orientation of female characters, which is also privileged in narrative description, is toward being-with-others. The village sizzles and steams with sound and smells of life, the urban neighbourhood draws newcomers into its 'shouting, laughing and cursing' (41), and in times of crisis, racial demarcations collapse in communal solidarity (140).

Appropriately, in a novel that catalogues the violent excesses of racial/political division, the central consciousness of Gem (through which the positive paradigm of communality is reflected) is revealed to be a blend of most of Guyana's ethnic groups. In-between racially, as she is in-between the temperaments of her parents, and in-between older sister and younger brother, Gem serves as a 'representative' subject for Nichols' project of weaving together personal and national history. She is a decentred subject, as open to other voices as is the narrative, where authorial reportage flows into dialogue, communal memory and free association within consciousness (see 21–24), in a style reminiscent of Brodber and Kincaid.

But this communal focus, this 'relational subjectivity' is not the only aspect of the novel where Bakhtin's 'carnival' tradition overlaps with feminist theory and what I've called a female/comic vision. There is also in *Whole of a Morning Sky*, and one might say throughout Nichols's writing, an emphasis on the body so persuasively argued for by Irigaray and other French feminist scholars. This is not to say that Nichols's fiction 'writes the body' in quite the way that Cixous suggests in her formulation of *écriture féminine*; although one *could* make a case for this text, in common with other West Indian fictions by women, being read for a kind of 'semiotic' patterning as a force *within* normal discourse. That is, one which is concerned with the bodily and material qualities of language, with creative excess rather than precise meaning, with fluidity, plurality, diffusion, sensuousness, open-endedness and, of course, playfulness.

However, if *Whole of a Morning Sky* does not necessarily 'write the female body', it certainly shares in the material, bodily principle that Bakhtin considers central to carnival imagery. Citing Boccaccio, Rabelais and Shakespeare, as well as classical and medieval 'carnival' literature, Bakhtin notes the frank concern with the human body, with its eating, drinking, defecating and sexual functions emphasized (1984: 18). Within the culture of folk humour, he perceives what he calls 'grotesque realism' in the representation of the body which (despite this term) is deeply positive. Again, the body is communal – the body of people – 'opposed to severance from the material and bodily roots of the world; it makes no pretence to renunciation of the earthy' (19). 'Grotesque' because 'exaggerated', the 'leading themes of these images of bodily life are fertility, growth, and a brimming-over abundance' (19) As with parody, grotesque realism 'lowers' (or reveals the other side of) 'all that is high, spiritual, ideal, abstract' (19) and turns the subject into flesh (20). Interestingly, nearly all of Bakhtin's favoured bodily images, which signify regeneration and the ever unfinished nature of corporeality, have to do with the female body: 'copulation, conception, pregnancy, and birth' (21). Like many male theorists, Bakhtin draws on woman's body for images of corporeality, implying that woman *is* her body; this rather essentialist premise can be seen to inform certain French feminist conceptions, for example, the notion of woman's fiction as 'writing the body' previously alluded to. However, it would be inappropriate to pursue this discussion here.

Bakhtin's carnival imagery, then, celebrates the body as a physical corrective to 'the narrow-minded seriousness of the spiritual pretence' (22); accepts its grotesque and mortal aspect as well as its 'gay principle of regeneration'; notes the body's integration with other bodies and that of the world (27); and comments on its incomplete, unfinished and thus eternally creative potential. I want to go on to explore some of these representations in *Whole of a Morning Sky*, but first it is important to call attention to a similar focus on the body by Edward Kamau Brathwaite as part of a West Indian female aesthetic, something he appears to have taken for granted as early as 1978 in his introduction to Hazel Campbell's *The Rag Doll and Other Stories*.

Brathwaite's 'forward' to the collection lauds the enriching contribution women have made to West Indian literature:

> And this immatriate influence is necessary, since the male principle by itself cannot conceptualize tomorrow. The male West Indian writer is still, on the whole, concerned with the stage or platform, box/ plantation, on (in) which we find ourselves; dominated by the aggressive sun, embattled by the wind of *isms*, finding romantic solace in the *id*: witch moon, night prostitute, the jasmine of the Other. 'Reality' is therefore too much noon or passion flower sunsets. (vi)

Here, Brathwaite notes the relegation, in male West Indian writing, of the female to Otherness ('witch moon', 'passion flower sunsets') that makes possible the norm of 'noon' (embattled engagement with the 'real' world of political and social flux). The sensibility of following Cixous 'masculine writing', that which embodies 'the male principle', is declamatory, enmeshed in aggressive conflict with nature and society, and articulates the solitary ego, the 'basic male-imagined Caribbean sense [is] of i/solation' (vii).

Therefore Brathwaite welcomes fictions like Campbell's which articulate the 'female principle' characterized, he claims, by a 'transformational quality' through which 'the creak of flesh becomes at last creative' (vi). Female flesh, female physical and social experience enters the text, thus transforming the literature. Brathwaite means less the anatomical body by this 'creak of flesh', I think, than what he terms 'the intransigent and feminine specific: domestic eye, domestic sense, domestic domination. And it is this twin and almost magic opposite which brings into our literature its new-found sense of matrix and maturity' (vi). Rather than seeing these comments in terms of a condescending nod to the kitchen sink, I'd suggest Brathwaite is here valorizing another 'little tradition' within the West Indian 'little tradition': a necessary writing in of physicality, sensuality, Bakhtin's eating, drinking, cooking, copulating and birthing body. It is this, Brathwaite feels, that accounts for the communal focus in West Indian 'feminine writing' in which he thinks 'there is a complementary sense of community which cuts across the [male?] ego-traps and weaves us back into the whole' (vii).

Of course, such comments can be accused of retaining a traditional male/female binarism. None the less, they support the kind of perspective I have attempted to describe in *Whole of a Morning Sky*'s female/comic vision, where woman's experience is set up in terms of its positive concern for maintaining life in opposition to the realm of 'anticomic' authority. The point is rather crudely made in Gem's parents' response to racial killing:

> Clara, protectress of human life that she was, recoiled from the brutality . . . [to which her husband's response is] 'Well, you're very naive when it comes to certain matters.'
>
> 'Naive?' said Clara. 'I bet you if men used to bring children into this world, they would have more respect for human life.' (139)

And indeed, in terms of its focus on the physical, sensual and domestic side of West Indian life, Nichols's novel conforms to Brathwaite's generalizations. There is recurrent mention of the 'basics' in the domestic sphere, and the work details women's practice of the sustaining arts by which life's necessities are supplied, against the odds. Ivy Payne supports her children quite literally (95) with blood and guts ('blood and runners' for the black pudding she sells) and communal festival ('what she made at her weekly Saturday night dances', (93)). Consequently, political strife is in all ways a threat to *life* for her and her children. It is Ivy and women like

her who wait for hours in the sun to get food, their basic priorities
reflecting on the upper-case rhetoric of the striker's placards: 'Workers
Will Die For Their Rights' (97). As it turns out, they do; the women's
families eat, and survive.

I don't mean to neatly oppose domestic and political priorities, since
domestic concerns in the novel also mirror national ones. Ivy's desire to be
economically independent of any man (95) and Clara's strategies for 'cutting and contriving' in the face of her husband's parsimony (87) parallel
efforts of the Guyanese people towards economic survival and self-determi-
nation. The point is, that Nichols's account of national history is told from
the domestic centre 'outwards'.

The festive resolution, the carnival celebration that is privileged in
comic vision, is expressed in the novel's periodic feasts, dances and wed-
dings, which subliminally re-enact the triumph of life over death. For
example, the Deepvali festival in the Walcott's neighbourhood is lovingly
detailed as a 'festival of goodwill' that brings together all races, classes,
ages and sexes in a 'social ritual' characterized by eating, drinking, music
and conversation. It stands in sharp contrast to the external noise of 'a bomb
explosion somewhere in the city' (127), suggesting the false logic of rever-
encing any ideology that supports bloodshed over such festivity.

The novel places 'home' as the matrix of life. Wilma's house is
perceived as a sanctuary from 'the frantic burning world' of the city
(110) and houses in the novel are places of safety and warmth and
intimacy. Gem and her girlfriend playing 'husband and wife' translate
domesticity into '[l]ying quietly together in a tangle of legs' (91) shut off
from the rest of the world; this is echoed in the image of Ivy Payne rising
early, gently hoisting herself 'over the sleeping limbs of her children'
(92). Unobtrusively, the novel prioritizes home, family, warmth, intimacy and love over aggression, conflict and strife that dominate the
socio-political sphere, to the detriment of the domestic. This makes the
intrusion of violence, unfortunately through male agents, all the more
reprehensible: Vibert's contemptible attack on his mother (93); Wilma's
husband's unreasonably tyrannical behaviour over, of all things, a plate
of roast pork (135)!

Women in their homes 'feed' the community. Clara's preparation of
African fufu and Indian curry – with a cup of 'English Red Rose Tea'
thrown in – both restates the ease of cultural integration at the domestic
level, and is described with almost erotic intensity:

> She kept up the rhythm with the long, smooth, thick pestle, up and
> down, round and round . . . Moist and magical, embodying at once all
> the diverse ingredients of her culture in this act of pounding fufu . . .
> (84)

The sensuous pleasures of taste and smell and texture, and the rhythmic pounding of pestle in mortar suggest the interconnection of bodily pleasures that women enable others to enjoy. These women are very much makers, creators – of children, edible commodities, clothing – and their activities centre around the domestic sphere, indicating its vital place within any notion of what 'makes' a nation.

In conclusion, I have suggested a female version of the carnivalesque, comic vision operating in *Whole of a Morning Sky* which undermines male authority, either through the exposure of certain icons sacred to patriarchy or in the (mostly gentle) deflation of affection and pompousness evidenced by male figures. This 'cutting down to size' disturbs the privileging of hierarchal patriarchal relations, which are shown to impinge negatively on the domestic/personal realm so crucial to human survival. The text can be read as celebrating instead a communal, integrative impulse via female agents. As the novel ends, with elections impending, the message of the second epigraph (by John Agard) warns against ignoring this impulse:

> an is all ahwe
> gon wake up an burn
> if we don't learn . . .
> if we don't learn . . .

Yet, eschewing a doom-laden closure that accurately mirrors what *did* result in Guyanese history, Nichols reaffirms the spirit of female community as Clara's friend from Highdam arrives, and the house echoes with women's laughter so that Archie feels for a moment as if they had never left the prelapsarian Eden (154).

Cyclical the novel may be, but not overly sentimental: no return to innocence is posited. What prevails is Gem's awareness of her growth, her maturity, and her firm link as woman with, as Bakhtin would have it, the 'body of the earth':

> The gooseberry tree laden with fat gooseberries,
> the pumpkins swelling big and heavy on the ground;
> the tomatoes ripe and plenty, and the bora climbing
> fresh and green as if it didn't care that the person
> who had planted it would be leaving. (156)

Departure from the carnival world, the green world does not preclude the transformative properties of the female/comic vision.

If Gem has the last word in *Whole of a Morning Sky*, I will let Bakhtin have the last here. The function of the 'carnivalesque' as well as its bodily imagery, in literature as elsewhere, is to consecrate inventive freedom, to permit the combination of a variety of different elements and their *rapprochement*, to liberate from the prevailing point of view of the world, from conventions and established truths, from clichés, from all that is . . . universally accepted. The carnival spirit offers the chance to have a new outlook on the world, to realize the relative nature of all that exists, and to enter a completely new order of things (1984: 34).

In effect, irreverence at the expense of 'respectability' and authoritarian posturing destablizes hegemonic discourse; emphasizing the material, the body, the 'domestic' focuses on the importance of an integrated, relational world view. If one accepts my contention that these are strategies employed within some West Indian fiction by women, then such strategies can be seen as having a transformative, if not revolutionary, impact upon patriarchal discourse. *Whole of a Morning Sky* can be read as a demonstration of Bakhtin's theorizing in practice, as the female body – like Teacher Mary's – disruptively makes its presence, and needs felt in the face of high-flown political rhetoric on 'justice', 'rights', 'rules' and the like, exposing them as useless and empty phrases in the particular context of articulation. The playfulness with which the text pokes fun at all forms of male officialdom does not detract from its pragmatic subversion of the primacy of patriarchal concepts of 'right' authority: it is, indeed, a West Indian 'woman version' with transformative attitude!

Notes

1   An apparently similar narrative strategy characterizes Merle Collin's novel *Angel*, where different socio-cultural perspectives (with their correspondingly various political alliances) are explored through the female protagonist's family members. However, in *Angel* (Seal Press, 1988; London: The Women's Press, 1988) the open consciousness of childhood soon becomes imbued with the mature protagonist/author's need to reshape events according to a particular ideology – to rewrite history.

CHAPTER 6 | 'Woman version': ideological theory

Political agendas

In the last five chapters I have discussed aspects of various literary theories which facilitate readings of female-authored texts as a 'woman version' on West Indian literature; readings, that is, which envision the texts as appropriating, echoing and subverting elements of 'master narratives' of all kinds, as versions which are not 'sub'- anything but, rather, woman-centred discourses that attend to a diverse range of voices and perspectives. Since the fiction itself is complex, inclusive and syncretic, then disparate theoretical inputs (including amalgams of these) can be suprisingly helpful in foregrounding its 'heteroglot', multivoiced, multistyled character. Obviously, if there *is* a West Indian female aesthetic, it is firmly situated within the cross-cultural creole ethos so important to the Caribbean, and shares its resistance to fixity and closure.

None of this is particularly novel or controversial. Yet attempts to theorize about West Indian women's writing, particularly its ideological orientations, sometimes meets with suspicion, if not hostility, from writers and readers of the literature. For example, in her report on the Second International Conference of Caribbean Women Writers, Sue Greene mentions a certain amount of 'wrangling' between authors and critics as to which group should be shown 'more deference', although the interdependence of the two was also acknowledged (534). This wrangling appeared to arise from more than competing egos, an unpleasant but often inevitable side effect of academic fora. To illustrate, Greene cites 'a well-established author' at the conference stating, 'I'm never coming back to one of these things. It's all about ideology. There's no discussion about art' (536). Presumably, this author had missed the many papers that dealt with what Greene terms 'comparative, psychological, colonialist, structuralist, and feminist readings of texts' (536). Surely a detailed 'reading' of a text, examining its mechanics, sources, influences and interpretations constitutes a 'discussion about art?' What seems to be at issue here is a perceived dichotomy between critical analysis that attends to ideological exegesis and one that examines literary technique alone.

Greene herself considers (536) that 'the relationship between art and ideology was not explored at the conference', a comment I find surprising. Explicitly or not, I think all critics would acknowledge that Caribbean women's writing is *crucially* informed by ideology, and reflect this in their analyses. Indeed, Eagleton (22) maintains that '[l]iterature, in the meaning of the word we have inherited, *is* an ideology. It has the most intimate relations to questions of social power'. For him, ideology consists of 'the ways in which what we say and believe connects with the power-structure and power-relations of the society we live in' (14). Caribbean women writers, perhaps more than most, inevitably interact with 'power-structures' in their societies (which happen to be post-colonial patriarchies) and this interaction implicitly shapes what they say in their art. Indeed, several women writers from the region are not only aware of the ideological nature of their work but recognize – as does Merle Hodge (1990: 202) – that 'there is no fundamental contradiction between art and activism.' Erna Brodber also specifies the 'activist intentions' of her writing (1990: 164). Lauretta Ngcobo's lines, which serve as an epigraph to an essay in *Motherlands* (290), are appropriate here:

> Out of our acrid neighbourhoods springs this rioting literature. It is not art for art's sake; its vibrance and immediacy are intended to forge unity and wrench a new identity.

Further, the fact that some critics choose to privilege Caribbean women's writing in their work implies that they consider such a project important: an ideological decision, surely? As Toril Moi points out (1991: 85), literary value judgments, being historically relative, are 'deeply imbricated in political value judgments.' All readings then, are in some sense political. A feminist reading – which is one obvious way of reading woman-centred literature from the Caribbean – acknowledges this fact and seeks to deconstruct oppositions between the political and aesthetic so that one is made 'aware of the politics of aesthetic categories as well as of the implied aesthetics of political approaches to art' (Moi, 1991: 86).

I would suggest that writers and readers do not so much resist the charge of ideology, as they resent being labelled according to a *specific* political affiliation. This applies particularly to the term 'feminist', which may be offensive to a writer who considers, often quite correctly, that her political context is not adequately represented in certain schools of 'international feminism'. Accordingly, I want to consider briefly four collections of stories published in the 1980s by Jamaican women to determine whether, in such a theoretically homogeneous group, specific feminist, or other, ideological positions are foregrounded.

I have chosen to focus on Senior's *Summer Lightning and Other Stories*, Campbell's *Woman's Tongue*, the Sistren Collective's *Lionheart Gal* and Adisa's *Bake Face and Other Guava Stories*. Both Senior and Adisa set their tales in rural and village Jamaica, while Campbell's scope is wider: the middle-class and peasant woman are represented, the suburb, slum and village are described. All the collections feature predominantly female characters, with *Lionheart Gal* focusing overwhelmingly on working-class women who have 'come to terms with difficulties in their personal lives' as they move 'from girlhood to adulthood, country to city, isolated individual experiences to more politicised collective awareness' (xiii).

In textualizing women's lives, their domestic, sexual and emotional concerns, and in demonstrating the necessary relation of this 'private' sphere to that of the economic and political, these collections can be said to qualify as 'feminist'. Indeed, such an impulse informs Campbell's text, which indicts women's complicity in their subjection, and the failure of communication between the sexes, as well as Adisa's celebration of the web of female relationships which are essential to her protagonists. Senior's exposure of the restrictive morality that binds girl children like Beccka and Lenora can be termed 'feminist', as can the testimonies of Sistren, which demonstrate awareness of their oppression as *women*; witness Foxy's understanding (253) that

> After we done talk ah get to feel dat di little day-to-day tings dat happen to we as women, is politics too. For instance, if yuh tek yuh pickney to hospital and it die in yuh hand – dat is politics. . . . If yuh man box yuh down, dat is politics. But plenty politicians don't tink dose tings have anyting to do wid politics.

The collections both describe women's subjugation as a result of sociohistorical factors, and celebrate their survival and transformational strategies in a society where unequal power relations are firmly entrenched. As such, they are texts that provide active support for, if not strident invitation of, a feminist reading.

However, such an ideological orientation has to be specific to the *West Indian* context, since, as is well known by now, Anglo-American and European feminisms have been guilty of theorizing that neglects important aspects of women's lives and fictional representations of women in the region, or is based on presuppositions that are problematic in the local context. Most feminist theory is now highly self-conscious of the dangers of speaking unilaterally *for* all women; to be ahistorical, essentializing or totalizing is to be seriously compromised in feminist scholarship.

Accordingly, Mordecai and Wilson (xii) observe that the short fiction collected in their anthology cannot be said to have straight feminist agendas since issues of gender are clearly bound up with issues of nationality, race and class. This holds true for the collections under review.

For one thing, the texts variously articulate an ideology of what I call, for want of a better term, 'cultural nationalism'. The fact that each of the writers employs a good deal of Jamaican Creole makes a political statement of confidence in this supposedly 'debased' indigenous language. The stories also take for granted that Jamaica has a dynamic and complex cultural life of its own, other than that imposed by colonialism. Certainly, neglected African survivals in the lives of the peasantry are highlighted; for example, in Adisa's mention of ancestral goddesses like Yemoja who must be pacified with libations (114), and of rituals used to counteract obeah and spirit possession by women like 'Miss Maud, the community myalist' (51–2).

Olive Senior's stories can also be read as articulating 'cultural nationalism' in that they subtly value the lifestyles of older, rural communities (emphasizing the role of elder women as memory of the group), and actively condemn a logic that endorses progress and modernity at the cost of contempt for one's origins; this is the point of the piece entitled 'Ascot'. However, Senior demonstrates the complexity of the issue. In 'Real Old Time T'ing', the search for 'roots' by urban Patricia translates into greedy acquisition of antiques; and such heirlooms represent to the villagers merely 'ol' bruk down furniture' which they are glad to sell off in order to 'go and trust plastic living room chair and aluminium dinette set' (61). None the less, a deep awareness of the past pervades Senior's text and resurfaces in the others: for example, Prudence in *Lionheart Gal* accounts for a dysfunctional father/daughter relationship in the light of slavery's heritage (111).

Any concern with history, personal or communal, is inextricably bound up, in the Jamaican context, with race/class hierarchies, and political attitudes as to race and class *are* expressed in different ways in the texts. Campbell, for example, simply observes wryly the different treatment accorded Miss Maud and Mrs Telfer in 'Supermarket Blues', while Adisa explicitly posits blackness as the norm of physical beauty: one character is ashamed of his 'red nega' colouring and desires 'to be purple-dark like the rest of them' (46). In contrast, the testimonies of *Lionheart Gal* often allude to the damaging effects that the preference for 'tall hair fair skin' features have on black women such as Doreen: 'Di whole heap a cussing bout how me black and ugly, only boots me now to say me a no notten' (99).

Senior's collection is both skilful and savage in its critique of race/class prejudice, frequently undermining the positive portrayal of the Jamaican peasantry by noting a debilitating internalization of Eurocentrism. So Myrtle in 'Bright Thursdays', who is seduced by the son of her employers, raises her illegitimate, and paternally unacknowledged, daughter to admire, imitate and aspire to the ways of the 'high estate' at the price of alienation from her own class and colour. Politically, Senior's text is a powerful protest against a belief system which leads a black woman to complain that

> everybody know this country going to the dog these days for is pure black people children they pushing to send high school. Anybody ever hear you can educate monkey? ('Ballad', 109–10)

Even in this brief overview, the limitations of feminisms which are based on fixed ideas about the nature of female experience, and the importance of differences between female-authored texts from varying racial and cultural contexts, should be apparent. Ideological orientations in West Indian women's writing cannot be trimmed to fit any neat paradigm as to *what* predominates in *which* group of writers. In these, as in most of the texts discussed in this book, a continuum of political directions operates, and exploration of ideological currents in the literature, feminist or otherwise, needs to be sensitively aware of intersecting agendas within the specifics of the text's cultural matrix.

Suspicion of theory

In addition to being wary of ideological containment, I think authorial unease with critical assessments also implies a resistance to *theoretical* containment, particularly by 'imported' literary theory. No doubt many readers would sympathize with Barbara Christian's reflection (xi) that 'when I read much literary criticism today, I wonder if the critic has read the book, since so often the text is but an occasion for espousing his or her philosophical [ideological/theoretical] point of view – revolutionary black, feminist or socialist programme.' While there is no doubt that there is *bad*, dogmatic criticism, one must still ask from what *other* perspective than 'his/ her point of view' can a critic speak? Indeed, the introduction from which this quote is taken itself constitutes a statement of Christian's own ideological/theoretical positions. After all, as Eagleton (194) reminds us, literary theory is 'indissociably bound up with political beliefs and ideological values'; in spite of any pretence at offering 'objective' or 'universal' insights, literary theories are based on particular doctrines relating to the interests of particular groups. The idea that there are 'non-political' forms of criticism, he insists, is simply a myth used to further certain political uses of literature all the more effectively (209).

What exactly are the objections raised to theory? Well, to start with, in the West Indies there is some distrust on the part of writers and readers of the typically off-putting jargon used by much post-structuralist criticism which suggests a kind of protected language of the initiate. Additionally, there is suspicion of the 'rarefied' nature that literary theory appears to have claimed for itself; after all, in the oral tradition stories are a part of everyday life, and don't need a separate 'scientific' language for discussing them. A related problem concerns the perception that local critics slavishly adopt 'foreign' theory without questioning its relevance to the local, or attending to equally valid methodologies developed 'at home'. As Slemon and Tiffin (1989: xix) note, this may account for Derek Walcott's instruction (1989: 141) to local academics – of which he is one – to beware 'the dead fish of French criticism', whose style he parodies unmercifully (despite claimimg to know nothing about it!): '"Moby Dick is nothing but words, and what are words, and what do I mean when I say Moby Dick, and if I say Moby Dick what exactly do I mean?"'

Further, Ashcroft, Griffiths and Tiffin note that theory, even the *concept* of theory, has been dismissed in some circles as 'irredeemably Eurocentric in its assumptions and political effect' (180); some feminists would also argue, along similar lines, that theoretical thinking is patriarchical thinking. And, of course, the dangers of theoretical reincorporation of literary texts have already been pointed out in Chapter 3. Abruna (1991: 278), citing Ketu Katrak's dismay at the appropriation of postcolonial works as 'raw material' for the production of literary theory, warns against 'prescriptive models' in interpreting West Indian women's fiction.

Lemuel Johnson (119) voices the common accusation that most well-known feminist critics 'focus on *white* women in literature and theory' while Sylvia Wynter (1990a: 355–6) rejects both 'feminism' and 'womanism' as critical concepts because of their Eurocentric bases, arguing instead the primacy of the variable 'race' in Caribbean women's writing. Sue Greene's conference report (537) includes Cliff Lashley's charge that 'international feminism' may do as much damage to this writing as Marxist criticism has done, suggesting that both discourses can be guilty of 'the sin of self-reflexive neo-colonialism. . . .' Indeed, Greene herself suggests (538) that 'for now, literary critics can best serve the study of Caribbean women's literature by expanding their concept of literature and by looking more deeply at the world from which it has arisen [?] than by applying critical theories of any kind.'

What emerges from such reservations is a concept of literary theory as an 'objective', universalizing, monolithic system, taking no account of local exceptions to its rules, a system which is unreflectingly adopted by critics and which, because it is Eurocentric and thus antithetical to the cultural and epistemological context of the Caribbean, has no insights of value to offer; instead, theory simply absorbs literary texts, regurgitating them as so much statistical evidence for its pronouncements. No wonder Caroline Rooney (101) images critical discourse as a colonising or imperialist discourse: one which annexes its textual object in order to perpetuate itself, institutionalize itself and its attendant ideological assumptions . . . [and] involves the subjection of not only the particular text but its 'world' or cultural and historical context to the homogenising standards and interests of the so-called 'first' world.

While not denying the validity of some of the objections raised, the general view of theory outlined above seems to me to ascribe a native 'passivity' to theoretical practitioners and literary texts in the Caribbean, an inability to engage with and, if necessary, resist dominating 'imported' critical models. When I use for my own ends some aspect of Kristevan theory, have I 'sold out' entirely to 'Western' feminism, willingly internalizing its hegemonic, and very likely, racist, foundations? Should I refuse to engage with the colonizing, monolithic monster of deconstruction at all, thus allowing its dominant discourse unopposed rule in the face of silence? And what of the texts: are they helpless to resist appropriation, having no inherent strategies for resisting heavy-handed manipulation by 'foreign' theory? Somehow, this scenario of powerlessness does not ring true.

Of course, the alternative view – that literary theory is both useful and manageable – has also been well documented. Rhoda Reddock, for example, takes on the indictment of feminism *per se* as an alien theoretical/ ideological phenomenon. Acknowledging (61) that in post-colonial territories hardly any 'other word in modern times has been so vilified for its European origins as *feminism*', she goes on to show that it is not a recent import into the Caribbean. Indeed, the 'modern women's movement in the English-speaking Caribbean is the continuation of a rich struggle for women's emancipation . . . firmly based within the sociopolitical and historical context of the region' (63). By feminism, she means 'the awareness of the subordination and exploitation of women in society and the conscious action to change that situation' (62); different feminists vary in their understanding of the problem and in the means necessary for the solution. For example, in the Caribbean the struggle for the amelioration of women has been traditionally linked to struggles for racial equality and human dignity (77). Sue Greene's reference (537) to Margaret Watt's presentation at the Trinidad conference (in fact, she means that of Belinda Edmonson) as the only one which 'analyzed with any thoroughness the concept of a peculiarly Caribbean feminism', none the less suggests that such an entity *exists*, and that feminist theory in the region is well on the way to indigenization.

Then there is the charge that contemporary 'Western' theory – postmodernism, deconstruction – ignores the material reality of the postcolonial situation, and is thus largely irrelevant. But Slemon and Tiffin (1989: x) point out that while, in practice, dominant forms of Anglo-

American post-structuralism retreat from geography and history into the realm of 'pure textuality', there are no *theoretical* constraints to the inclusion of such social materiality (that is, actual determinants of gender, race, class and cultural difference) in accounting for literary production and consumption. Indeed, as Ashcroft, Griffiths and Tiffin observe (165), much contemporary European criticism tends to 'dismantle assumptions about language and textuality and to stress the importance of ideological construction in socio-textual relations . . . .' So, as noted, do post-colonial texts, suggesting that the 'concerns of these discourses are therefore increasingly interactive and mutually influential' (165).

Further, both 'Caribbean feminist' and deconstructive approaches share an insistence on questioning the received order, exploring political and other structures that support the dominant discourse, not least by interrogating the necessary rightness of binary opposites (man as presence/woman as lack). Finally, can theoretical orientations like deconstruction – which holds central the tenet that *all* discourses, including theoretical ones, contain the seeds of their own destabilization – be fairly accused as inherently monolithic and universalizing?

This leads on to the objection to theory as an alien, 'objective', scientific knowledge which may be at odds with the epistemology of some cultures, especially in oral societies. However, it seems to me that where contemporary European, post-colonial and 'Caribbean feminist' theory overlap is in a constant investigation and relativizing of *all* 'ways of knowing'. Bill Ashcroft (25), for example, questions the whole notion of an essentially female or 'authentic' national language/identity, positing instead that in a creole culture, the constant process of syncretism works to evade attempts at defining 'uniquely distinguishing characteristics'. Going further, he suggests that this 'openness to the continuing deferral of cultural identity' (33) – the constant play between, say, race, class, gender, caste and class markers – leads to a consideration of the term 'female' (like 'national') as a fundamentally *arbitrary* designation, preparing the way for full recognition of plurality and multiplicity rather than 'objective', scientific categorization.

Toril Moi (1986: 212–14) makes a similar point, citing Kristeva's *refusal* to define femininity as a necessary defence against essentialism. Instead, femininity is considered (as could 'Caribbean', 'Third World') as 'that which is marginalised by the patriarchal symbolic order' (212). Again, we see the insistence in contemporary theoretical orientations on the *relativity* of judgment: 'What is perceived as marginal at any given time depends on the position one occupies' (213). When women (or blacks) are marginally positioned in the symbolic order, and construed by patriarchy (or Eurocentrism) as the limit, the border-line of that order – *both* necessary frontier between civilized man and chaos *and* merging with that chaos outside – they can be represented in fiction as possessing a pure innocent nature *and* as the 'heart of darkness.' Neither, of course, is *essentially* true of blacks/women (213); but only attention to the 'ways of knowing' that constructed them as such can de-privilege epistemologies and question fundamental presuppositions generally held to be 'true'.

Importantly, however, Moi introduces a practical note when she discusses Kristeva's refusal of the binary opposition of male/female as a matter of metaphysics: for 'as long as patriarchy is dominant, it still remains *politically* essential for feminists to defend women *as* women in order to counteract the patriarchal oppression that precisely despises women *as* women' (214). In other words, one can balance a radically transformative theoretical awareness of the metaphysical nature of gender identities (in order to avoid 'an inverted form of sexism', or essentialism) with conscious political awareness of gender inequality.

Hazel Carby (16), noting that black feminist theory shares a 'structural and conceptual pattern of questions and issues with other modes of feminist inquiry', insists on the rejection of 'essential and ahistorical' reliance for definition simply on common experience. Carby too, calls for a theory that focuses on multiplicity and plurality, 'a feminist critical practice that pays particular attention to the articulation of gender, race and class' in 'the cultural production of black women intellectuals' (17). Like Moi, her work repudiates simplistic categorizations of identity – '[b]lack feminist criticism has too frequently been reduced to an experiential relationship that exists between black women as critics and black women as writers who represent black women's reality' (16) – while remaining rooted in a 'materialist account' of the 'social relations' that inscribe black women.

Finally, the colonizing intentionality of 'imported' theory, aided by the na(t)ive critic who absorbs and disseminates 'foreign' perspectives, and by the literary text itself – a malleable entity – needs to be addressed. The assumption is that the local critic applies theory exactly as she or he receives it; surely this is virtually impossible? As Ashcroft, Griffiths and Tiffin (180) remind us, in practice *critical* texts 'as well as creative texts are products of post-colonial hybridity' and *The Empire Writes Back* cogently demonstrates how indigenous theoretical practices interact and overlap with other models. Critics in the Caribbean don't simply *assume* the truth of 'imported' theory but adapt and modify it, argue against it, and force it into counter-discursive roles. Arun Mukherjee actually practises what she preaches (45) in her article, arguing the need to 'dismantle the prison hold of binaries and work for theoretical perspectives that can come to grips with the pluralistic and heterogeneous nature of the 'socio-ideological' discourse of post-colonial cultures.'

In addition, it can be argued that certain theories – feminism and post-colonialism, for example – are essentially anti-authoritarian, and tend to be wary of reincorporating texts into intellectual orthodoxy (Ashcroft, 24). However, even if we do see theory misused as a 'colonizing' force, Caroline Rooney (112–15) shows that texts *can* resist appropriation, assimilation into critical orthodoxy by, for example, parodying the critical stance and thus pre-empting interpretation, or refusing to privilege and exclude categories. She demonstrates that certain women's texts constantly and unpredictably revise themselves, reworking meanings and creating paradoxes that are not necessarily contradictions (118). The text, then, retains a certain amount of 'agency', and is able to interrogate that which seeks to interrogate it for specific theoretical data (121).

Claire Harris's strong statement of herself as a writer who refuses appropriation and assimilation (306–9) is matched by the critical practice of scholars like Susheila Nasta, who insist that creative dialogue between theoretical currents and literary texts *can* exist: 'Western feminist theories current in "First World" audiences need not simply appropriate these writings to elucidate their biases but . . . can "illuminate" the texts' (xvi–xvii). Indeed, she feels the give-and-take, the 'double discourse . . . often at work between the cultural values encoded in the text itself and the individual critic's particular cultural baggage' (xvii), can be a mutually educational experience.

So much for the pros and cons of 'borrowing' from theory. I am aware of some of the difficulties and inherent contradictions here. For example, in defending my appropriation of theory, I might be seen as endorsing my own appropriation *by* theory! Again, I am probably guilty of being what Slemon and Tiffin (1989: xviii) term 'excessively affiliative in citation' of other critics, particularly Ashcroft, Griffiths, Tiffin and Slemon! There does not seem to be any method of engaging in theoretical debate that doesn't run such risks, and where I find critical work, *as applied to the specific West Indian literary context* in which women's writing is situated, both methodologically useful and politically sympathetic, I do of course use it. Still, such citation can and, no doubt, will be perceived as a need to endorse my own readings with officially recognized ('foreign') stamps of approval.

Further, my casual use of terms like 'woman', 'female', 'race', 'history' and 'experience', without constant definition and redefinition – particularly in the light of Diana Fuss's reminder (1989) of the continuing 'essentialism' versus 'constructionism' debate – is likely to be targeted by those who, *pace* Walcott (1989: 141), insist that 'it all depends on what you mean by. . . .'

Another risk implicit in the kind of theoretical syncretism I suggest, is the possibility of 'watering down' or splitting political priorities. For example, in combining some strategies of post-colonial and feminist theory, Chandra Mohanty's insistence (1988: 73) that sexual difference is not in itself coterminus with female subordination – that power is not simply defined in terms of men who have and women who don't – must be admitted. At the same time, I have tried to avoid subsuming textual representation of women's subordination *qua* women, to that of their oppression as colonized/non-white/working class. In other words, I want to focus on how gender issues are complicated by issues of race, class and nationality rather than on how the latter *eclipse* the former.

Finally, as a teacher of West Indian literature, it is always important to privilege the literary text, and a book on 'theoretical orientations' runs the risk of at least partially directing readers away from fiction towards critical scholarship. Considering the growing preponderance of theoretical courses in contemporary academic institutions, it is important to reiterate here that literary works come first. One way of transcending this dilemma is to consider the work being done by post-colonial and feminist scholars on literary texts *as* theoretical paradigms. I referred to Tiffin's study of *Myal* in Chapter 4, and recent papers by Donnell and Tiffin (1992) continue this approach.

Donnell addresses the writing of Jamaica Kincaid as theory; specifically, as writing which demonstrates the limitations of certain theories when applied to West Indian female-authored texts. Tiffin (1992) treats *Wide Sargasso Sea* and Naipaul's *Guerillas* as not only thematizing English textual containment and the inscription of the colonized within imperial narrative, but also suggesting theoretical models for escaping this enclosure, largely through disobedient localized readings of texts within the framework of an indigenous interpretive community. Michael Dash (26) argues that Caribbean literature in its 'radical questioning of the need to totalize, systematize and control' is in fact inherently 'deconstructionist', and has been for some time.

Further, his claim that the Caribbean writer valorizes 'latency, formlessness and plurality', suggests another textual strategy for blocking appropriation: given no monolithic textual discourse but rather a complex and interwoven network of discursive positions, interpretive conclusions are necessarily qualified and deferred. Pauline Melville's *Shape-Shifter*, a recent (1990) award-winning collection of stories, suggests itself as a 'paradigmatic theoretical text' in this respect. Mervyn Morris (1992: 2) comments on the Anancy-like, protean nature of 'the author', and the way the extensive range of subject matter and narrative experiment, as well as a certain 'cross-cultural open-endedness' (10), makes for multiple readings. I have suggested in this chapter, the simplistic nature of attempting to label West Indian women's fictions according to ideological focus solely on race/class, gender or other issues. *Shape-Shifter* is an exemplum of skilful interweaving of sexual, regional, racial and other politics, which as we see, cannot be neatly polarized in the West Indian context and even less so in this text, which situates the West Indies in relation to England, and sometimes 'in' the metropole: 'I couldn't believe that I had lived in my ground floor London flat for five years without even realising that Jamaica was just on the other side of my back wall' (111).

Melville prevents us taking anything for granted; with Kincaid and Brodber, she blurs boundaries of time and space and narrative centrality. More importantly, she deconstructs the easy adversarial status that too often informs political rhetoric. The story, 'You Left the Door Open', complicates the superficial binarism of aggressive male versus passive female victim in a chilling account of paranormal rape (by whom? of whom?). And in 'The Conversion of Millicent Vernon', racial distinctions and the hostilities they engender are subverted by reference to the 'genetic kaleidoscope' that results from racial mixing in the West Indies, so that with each generation 'a greater variety of ghosts [ancestors] appeared, sometimes as many as four or five mischievously occupying one body' (28). What *Shape-Shifter* casually posits, is a concept of the writer/reader/character as a site of multiple and heterogeneous 'subject-positions', emphasizing not so much what Fuss (34) describes as a 'phone book compiling of "I-slot" listings', but 'the fluid boundaries and continual commerce between them'. Such a fictional procedure, probably influenced by the work of Wilson Harris, works against simplistic theoretical ideological readings.

'In order to survive,' comments Dash (26), 'the Caribbean sensibility must spontaneously decipher and interpret the sign systems of those who wish to dominate and control.' Several West Indian texts by women demonstrate such a sensibility in their slippery evasion of dogmatic readings and theoretical labelling, and are thus powerful theoretical and ideological resources for the concerned critic.

Woman version

I would like to conclude with one more reiteration: that the processes by which the dub version comes into being, processes for which I see analogies in West Indian women's writing, have material bases in the hybrid nature of creole Caribbean culture, as described by Brathwaite (1971 and subsequently). Despite my quibbles with Brathwaite in Chapter 1, what I perceive as his notion of 'interculturation' – that is, no *one* group, race, religion, class or gender has a monopoly on *the* West Indian experience – is clearly crucial to my account of a 'woman version'. In Caribbean cultures, as in their Creole languages, European 'lexifiers' may change out of all recognition; new inputs (from the Americas, India, Syria, China) may produce new formations; indigenous cultural forms (Rastafarianism, calypso, reggae, dub) may contribute new rhythms and constructions. Thus such cultures, like their languages, can only be understood as developing systems that constantly elude the imposition of rigid fixity and categorization. Such cultures/languages/literatures, then, are recognizably West Indian yet are never static, and attempts to sift and isolate the ingredients of the 'callaloo', however fascinating, are thankless and/or futile if guided by prescriptive notions about finding 'the' source.

This 'creole ethos' I have kept paramount in my consideration of the writing. So have other critics. Nasta (xvi) highlights the 'positive effects of the cross-fertilization and creolization of cultures and languages that define the syncretic nature of the Caribbean literary tradition' on which women's fiction 'versions'. Balutansky (1990: 549), reviewing *Out of the Kumbla*, considers that the collection of essays 'documents important progress in the effort to articulate the relation between cultural "creolization" and the "creolized" or "ecletic" form of Caribbean women's writing.' Ashcroft, Griffiths and Tiffin note that in a situation of cultural hybridity, various discourses of marginality (by race, gender, psychological 'normalcy' and so on) 'intersect in a view of reality which supersedes the geometric distinction of centre and margin and replaces it with a sense of the complex, interweaving and syncretic accretion of experience' (104). Given this creole ethos, they see a certain 'creole logic' in theorizing about the literature: 'it is possible to argue that post-colonial discourse may appropriate what it requires from European theory' (168). And this is precisely what I have been trying to do in this book.

As far as the 'woman version' of West Indian literature is concerned, several critics are working, in different ways, toward a similar theoretical position, one which paradoxically refuses easy definition. Fido's model of a crossroads space (1990: 30) from which writers and critics choose directions and chart their own paths, is similar to the model suggested by Claudia Tate (xvi) and echoes Mordecai and Wilson's description of the 'complex of . . . criss-crossing valuings' (xiii) that characterizes Caribbean women's fiction. Paravisini-Gebert (1992: 66) describes several francophone texts by Caribbean women as 'standing on the crossroads where issues of race, gender, class and power converge. . . .'

Others stress the inclusiveness of a woman-centred literary tradition in the region. Balutansky (1990) argues that there can never be one single 'authentic' Caribbean voice, female or otherwise, and generalizations about Caribbean female identity must recognize the centrality of *diversity*. Like other scholars, she calls attention to the variety of voices and styles in literature by women of the region, since women 'may share a common history of colonialism, and many other experiences, but the interplay of these various heritages creates a new turn' in the way they each experience their world (546). Pamela Mordecai's 'prismatic form', an exciting concept she has been refining for some time, speaks to the type of inclusiveness described above. For Mordecai (1986), 'prismatic conscious-ness' is the disposition to perceive and construe experience in terms of (sometimes unresolved) pluralities, 'th[is] impulse to pluralities [being usually] restrained by a manner of knowing essentially linear' as she explains in her forward to *Out of the Kumbla* (viii). Mordecai feels that such a refraction of experience and perception, one that pays attention to the *multi-faceted* nature of perception, is an important feature of Carib-bean women's writing, which owes much to the reality of syncretism in Caribbean societies. The fascinating way in which women writers slide across codes and registers of language, she notes, is one aspect of this many-sided vision.

What is evident here is an awareness of and attention to the dub version, to a special sense of inclusive, fluid diversity in Caribbean writing by women. Davies and Fido's introduction to *Out of the Kumbla* (17) notes a similar plurality in critical methodology among the contributors who are 'engaged multiple-voicedly with both the female condition and its affirma-tion as well as the critique of the politics of imperialism and marginalization' (18).

To return briefly to the question of ideology. I have argued that, considered as a group, West Indian female-authored texts follow divergent ideological trajectories and pursue what can be perceived as conflicting options. If the writers occupy multiple 'subject positions', so do critics as far as theoretical approaches are concerned. The literature can accommo-date ideological/theoretical pluralism, and such readings are rewarding. But to be 'rewarding' suggests, for me, a further underlying political criterion: those readings are *most* 'rewarding' that serve to articulate the voices of silenced, marginalized and oppressed women, and their calls for strategies of empowerment. As suggested in Chapter 3, both post-colonial and femi-nist theories share such a political motivation. Ashcroft, Griffiths and Tiffin (177) elaborate on the way the two discourses 'are oriented towards the future, positing societies in which social and political hegemonic shifts have occurred'; both 'link a disruptive involvement in books with a project towards revolutionary disruption in society at large' (177). Theory, as noted, is informed by ideology, and this should determine how we use it for specific political ends.

As I read them, West Indian women writers – *Caribbean* women writers – are implicitly committed to an ideology of change, to the necessity for exposing and subverting inequalities in their societies and, sometimes, suggesting ways in which transformations might come about. Their fiction *also* transforms consciousness, communicating a certain 'way of knowing' that deconstructs oppositionals on which imperial and patriarchal power largely depend for power. In their writing we see, with Rhys, that 'there is always the other side. Always.' I also feel that most critics who read and study and teach this literature share the ideological goals of the writers *as well as* the irreverent 'deconstructive' approach which can adopt and adapt theoretical methodologies at will in the service of such a goal.

Recognizing this unity-in-diversity, and given the multicultural, syncretic nature of regional life and language, as well as the disparate voices and songs of Caribbean women writers (the products, after all, of this eclectic and polyphonic culture), I have put forward a case for theoretical experimentation. Understandably, writers distrust misused or rigidly appropriative criticism; such 'colonizing' tendencies are repugnant to a fictional discourse that embraces pluralities and to which complexity is fundamental. So, rather than attempt to construct one theoretical model or another, I have suggested the need for modified and/or synthetic theoretical approaches which can and do take account of the multiplicity, complexity, and the intersection of apparently conflicting orientations which we find in the writing. As Moi (1991: 87) notes, feminists have politicized almost all existing critical methods and approaches; as theorists of Caribbean literature by women, a similar policy of unapologetic indigenizing appropriation might be recommended, an approach which combines methodological heterogeneity *and* ideological commonality while refusing to be ultimately formalized, boxed, labelled under any one 'ism'.

Olive Senior's story 'Lily, Lily' (1989: 144–5) closes with the sound of women's voices, silenced for a long time, singing *together*: their own 'woman version', shared by a communal audience, against that which the 'proper' Miss Emmeline Greenfield, with her 'superior knowledge' would impose. At the same time, Emmeline's version is implicitly (parodically) a part of their song, yet another strand in this richly braided narrative. I can't think of any better way of ending this book than by giving Senior's celebratory voices a hearing:

> From inside the house comes first the sound of a piano (badly out of tune) then the clear, unmistakable sound of Lily's voice not heard for over a dozen years. We had forgotten its beauty so cannot compare it now to what it was. We just close our eyes and let ourselves soar with Lily's song.
>
> But what is this? Are there two Lilies now? For softly, softly, faintly at first, comes another voice, piercingly sweet as a child's, joining our Lily's, getting stronger and more assured as it sings a descant to our Lily's song. Two voices, perfectly matched, perfectly blended. Can there be a sweeter sound in the world than Lily, Lily singing?
>
> O if only that Emmeline Greenfield with her superior knowledge acquired from books, with her formidable social inheritance, with her elegant turn of phrases (in foreign languages too), if only she

were here to give to the world a truly inspired version of this magical
moment. What a story she would tell!

Bibliography of works cited

Primary sources

Adisa, Opal Palmer (1986) *Bake Face and other Guava Stories*, Berkeley: Kelsey St Press.

Allfrey, Phyllis Shand (1982) *The Orchid House*, London: Virago. First published 1953.

Bliss, Eilot (1984) *Luminous Isle*, London: Virago. First published 1934.

Brodber, Erna (1980) *Jane and Louisa Will Soon Come Home*, London: New Beacon.

— (1988) *Myal*, London: New Beacon.

Brown, Stewart (ed.) (1990) *Caribbean New Wave: Contemporary Short Stories*, London: Heinemann.

Campbell, Hazel D. (1983) *Woman's Tongue*, Kingston: Savacou.

Carmichael, Mrs (1969) *Domestic Manners and Social Condition of the White, Coloured and Negro Population of the West Indies*, New York: Negro Universities Press. First published 1833. 3 vols.

Carter, Martin (1977) *Poems of Succession*, London: New Beacon.

Cassin, Freida (c.1896) *With Silent Tread*, Antigua: G.A. Uphill.

Cliff, Michele (1980) *The Land of Look Behind*, New York: Firebrand Books.

— (1984) *Abeng*, New York: Crossing Press.

— (1987) *No Telephone to Heaven*, New York: Dutton.

Collins, Merle (1988) *Angel*, London: The Women's Press.

Condé, Maryse (1987) *La Vie Scélérate*, Paris: Editions Seghers.

Edgell, Zee (1982) *Beka Lamb*, London: Heinemann.

Fenwick, Eliza (1927) *The Fate of the Fenwicks: Letters to Mary Hays (1798–1828)* (ed.) A.F. Wedd. London: Methuen.

Gilroy, Beryl (1986) *Frangipani House*, London: Heinemann.

Goodison, Lorna (1986) *I Am Becoming My Mother*, London and Port of Spain: New Beacon.

—(1988) *Heartease*, London and Port of Spain: New Beacon.

— (1990) *Baby Mother and the King of Swords: Short Stories*, London: Longman.

Hodge, Merle (1981) *Crick Crack Monkey*, London: Heinemann. First published 1970.

Jenkin, Henrietta Camilla (1859) *Cousin Stella; or, Conflict*, London: Smith and Elder.

Kincaid, Jamaica (1984) *Annie John*, London: Pan.

— (1990) *Lucy*, New York: Farrar, Straus and Giroux.

Lockett, Mary (1902) *Christopher, a novel*, New York: Abbey Press.

Long, Gabrielle Margaret Vere Campbell [Joseph Shearing] (1936) *The Golden Violet; the story of a Lady Novelist*, London: Heinemann.

Lynch, Mrs Henry (1847) *The Cotton Tree, or Emily, The Little West Indian*, London: John Hatchard.

— (1848) *The Family Sepulchre: A Tale of Jamaica*, London: Seelys.

— (1865) *Years Ago: A Tale of West Indian Domestic Life of the Nineteenth Century*, London: Jarrold and Sons.

McKenzie, Alecia (1992) *Satellite City and Other Stories*, London and Kingston: Longman.

Marsh-Caldwell, Anne (1850) *Adelaide Lindsay; a novel*, London: Cox and Wyman. 3 vols.

Marshall, Paule (1959) *Brown Girl, Brownstones*, New York: Avon Books.

— (1969) *The Chosen Place, The Timeless People*, New York: Harcourt, Brace and World.

— (1983) *Praisesong for the Widow*, London: Virago.

Melville, Pauline (1990) *Shape-Shifter*, London: The Women's Press.

Morris, Mervyn (ed.) (1990) *Contemporary Caribbean Short Stories*, London and Boston: Faber.

Nichols, Grace (1986) *Whole of a Morning Sky*, London: Virago.

Nugent, Maria (1966) *Lady Nugent's Journal of her residence in Jamaica from 1801 to 1805* (ed.) Philip Wright, Kingston: Institute of Jamaica. First published 1907; first printed in England for private circulation 1839.

Patrick-Jones, Marion (1976) *Jou'vert Morning*, Port-of-Spain: Columbus Publishers.

Philip, Marlene Nourbese (1989) *She Tries Her Tongue: Her Silence Softly Breaks*, Charlottetown: Ragweed Press.

— (1991) *Looking for Livingstone: An Odyssey of Silence*, Toronto: The Mercury Press.

Phillips, Caryl (1991) *Cambridge*, London: Bloomsbury.

Pollard, Velma (1988) *Crown Point and Other Poems*, Leeds: Peepal Tree Press.

— (1989) *Considering Woman*, London: The Women's Press.

Rhys, Jean (1968) *Wide Sargasso Sea*, Harmondsworth: Penguin. First published 1966.

Prince, Mary (1987) *History of Mary Prince, a West Indian Slave, related by Herself*, In Henry Louis Gates, Jr. (ed.) *The Classic Slave Narratives*, New York: New American Library. First published 1831.

Ramchand, Kenneth (ed.) (1982) *Best West Indian Stories*, London: Nelson Caribbean.

Riley, Joan (1985) *The Unbelonging*, London: The Women's Press.

Salkey, Andrew (ed.) (1960) *West Indian Stories*, London: Faber.

Seacole, Mary (1984) *The Wonderful Adventures of Mary Seacole in Many Lands*, (Second ed.) Introd. Ziggi Alexander and Audrey Dewjee. London: Falling Wall Press. First published 1857.

Selvon, Samuel (1984) *Moses Ascending*, London: Heinemann. First published 1975.

Senior, Olive (1985) *Talking of Trees*, Kingston: Calabash.

— (1986) *Summer Lightning and Other Stories*, London: Longman.

— (1989) *Arrival of the Snake Woman and Other Stories*, London: Longman.

Shinebourne, Janice (1986) *Timepiece*, Leeds: Peepal Tree Press.

Sistren, with Honor Ford-Smith (1986) *Lionheart Gal*, London: The Women's Press.
Stephenson, Clarine (1911) *Undine: An Experience*, New York: Broadway Publishing Co.
Symonett, Ethel Maud (1895) *Jamaica: Queen of the Carib Sea*, Kingston: Mortimer C. De Souza.
Thomas, Elean (1991) *The Last Room*, London: Virago.
Warner-Viera, Miriam (1982) *As the Sorcerer Said*, London: Longman. First published 1980.
Wynter, Sylvia (1962) *The Hills of Hebron*, New York: Simon and Schuster.

Secondary sources

Abel, Elizabeth (1979) 'Women and Schizophrenia: the fiction of Jean Rhys', *Contemporary Literature*, XX, 2 (Spring): 155–77.
Abruna, Laura Niesen de (1990) 'Twentieth-Century Women Writers from the English-Speaking Caribbean', in Cudjoe (ed.): 86–97.
— (1991) 'Family Connections: Mother and Mother Country in the Fiction of Jean Rhys and Jamaica Kincaid', in Nasta (ed.): 257–89.
Alleyne, Mervyn (1980) *Comparative Afro-American: An Historical Comparative Study of the English-based Afro-American Dialects of the New World*, Ann Arbor: Karoma.
Anderson, Paula (1981) 'Jean Rhys' *Wide Sargasso Sea*: The Other Side/Both Sides Now', in Similowitz and Knowles (eds): 237–59.
Ashcroft, W.D. (1989) 'Intersecting Marginalities: Post-Colonialism and Feminism', *Kunapipi*, 11, 2: 23–35.
Ashcroft, Bill, Gareth Griffiths and Helen Tiffin (1989) *The Empire Writes Back: Theory and Practice in Post-Colonial Literatures*, London and New York: Routledge.
Baker, Houston A., Jr. (1984) *Blues, Ideology, and Afro-American Literature: A Vernacular Theory*, Chicago: University of Chicago Press.
Bakhtin, Mikhail (1984) *Rabelais and His World*, Trans. Hélène Iswoksky, Bloomington: Indiana University Press. First published 1966.
— (1988) 'From the prehistory of novelistic discourse', in David Lodge (ed.) *Modern Criticism and Theory: A Reader*, London and New York: Longman: 125–56. First published 1967.
Balutansky, Kathleen M. (1990) 'Naming Caribbean Women Writers: A Review Essay', *Callaloo*, 13, 3 (Summer): 539–50.
— (Forthcoming) 'Redefining "Female Identity" in Contemporary Anglophone and Francophone Fiction by Caribbean Women', in A. James Arnold (ed.) ICLA *New Literary History of the Caribbean*, Amsterdam and Philadelphia: Benjamins.
Baugh, Edward ed. (1978) *Critics on Caribbean Literature*, London: George Allen and Unwin.
— (1981) 'Edward Brathwaite as Critic', in Smilowitz and Knowles (eds): 95–115.
Beckles, Hilary (1989) *Natural Rebels: A Social History of Enslaved Black Women in Barbados*, London: Zed Books.
— (forthcoming) 'White Women and Slavery in the Caribbean', *History Workshop Journal*, (special issue, due 1993).
Berrian, Brenda F. (1989) *Bibliography of Women Writers from the Caribbean (1831–1986)*, Washington: Three Continents Press.

Boehmer, Elleke (1991) 'Stories of Women and Mothers: Gender and Nationalism in the Early Fiction of Flora Nwapa', in Nasta (ed.): 3–23.

Brathwaite, Edward Kamau (1963) 'Roots: a commentary on West Indian Writers', *Bim*, 10, 37 (July/December): 10–21.

—(1967–68) 'Jazz and the West Indian Novel', *Bim*, 45: 275–84 and 39–51; *Bim*, 46: 115–26.

— (1969) 'Caribbean Critics', *Critical Quarterly*, 11, 3 (Autumn): 268–76.

— (1970) 'West Indian Prose Fiction in the Sixties: A Survey', *Caribbean Quarterly*, 16, 4 (December): 5–17.

— (1971) *The Development of Creole Society in Jamaica 1770–1820*, Oxford: Clarendon Press.

— (1974) *Contradictory Omens*, Mona, Kingston: Savacou.

— (1978) Introduction to Hazel Campbell's *The Rag Doll and Other Stories*, UWI, Mona, Kingston: Savacou: vi–vii.

Breiner, Laurence A. (1992) 'On the Road to the New Imperialism', Paper to the Ninth Triennial ACLALS Conference, UWI, Mona, Kingston (August 13–20).

Brodber, Erna (1982) *Perceptions of Caribbean Women: Towards a Documentation of Stereotypes*, Cave Hill, Barbados: ISER.

— (1982) Interviewed by Evelyn O'Callaghan, Kingston: n.p. (April 7).

— (1990) 'Fiction in the Scientific Procedure', in Cudjoe (ed.): 164–18.

Brown, Bev E.L. (1986) 'Mansong and Matrix: A Radical Experiment', in Peterson and Rutherford (eds): 68–79.

Bush, Barbara (1990) *Slave Women in Caribbean Society 1650–1838*, Kingston: Heinemann; London: James Currey; Bloomington: Indiana University Press.

Campbell, Elaine (1978) 'Report from Dominica, BWI' *World Literature Written in English*, 17: 305–16.

Carby, Hazel V. (1989) *Reconstructing Womanhood: The Emergence of the Afro-American Woman Novelist*, Oxford and New York: Oxford University Press. First published 1987.

Cassidy, F.G. and R.B. LePage (eds) (1980) *Dictionary of Jamaican English*, Second ed., Cambridge: Cambridge University Press. First published 1967.

Chesler, Phyllis (1972) *Women and Madness*, New York: Avon.

Christian, Barbara (1985) Introduction to *Black Feminist Criticism: Perspectives on Black Women Writers*, New York: Pergamon Press: ix–xv.

Cliff, Michelle (1990) 'Clare Savage as a Crossroads Character', in Cudjoe (ed.): 263–8.

Cobham, Rhonda (1982) '"Getting out of the Kumbla": review of *Jane and Louisa Will Soon Come Home*', *Race Today*, (December 1981–January 1982) 34.

— (1990) 'Women in Jamaican Literature 1900–1950', in Davies and Fido (eds): 195–222.

Cooper, Carolyn (1989) 'Writing Oral History: Sistren Theatre Collective's *Lionheart Gal*', *Kunapipi*, 11, 1: 49–57.

— (1990) 'Afro-Jamaican Folk Elements in Brodber's *Jane and Louisa Will Soon Come Home*', in Davies and Fido (eds): 279–88.

— (1991) ' "Me Know No Law, Me Know No Sin": Transgressive Identities and the Voice of Innocence in Selected Female-Centred Jamaican Oral Texts', Paper to the Tenth Annual Conference on West Indian Literature, UWI, St Augustine.

— (1991) '"Something Ancestral Recaptured": Spirit Possession as Trope in Selected Feminist Fictions of the African Diaspora', in Nasta (ed.): 64–87.

— (1992) '"The Great Man Can No Longer Just Get up and Go": Jamaica Kincaid, Christopher Columbus and the Paralysis of Patriarchy', Paper to Third International Conference of Caribbean Women Writers, Curaçao (July 27–31).

Covi, Giovanna (1990) 'Jamaica Kincaid and the Resistance to Canons', in Davies and Fido (eds): 345–54.

Craig, Christine (1984) '*Wonderful Adventures of Mrs Seacole in Many Lands*: Autobiography as literary genre and a window to character', *Caribbean Quarterly*, 30, 2: 33–47.

Crosta, Suzanne (1992) 'Narrative and Discursive Strategies in Maryse Condé's *Traversée de la Mangrove*', *Callaloo*, 15, 1: 147–55.

Cudjoe, Selwyn (1985) 'Maya Angelou and the Autobiographical Statement', in Evans (ed.): 6–24.

— (ed.) (1990) *Caribbean Women Writers: Essays from the First International Conference*, Wellesley, Massachusetts: Calaloux.

D'Costa, Jean (1986) 'Jean Rhys (1890–1979)', in Dance (ed.): 390–404.

— (1990) 'Bra Rabbit meets Peter Rabbit: Genre, Audience, and the Artistic Imagination: Problems in Writing Children's Fiction', in Cudjoe (ed.): 254–62.

Dance, Daryl (ed.) (1986) *Fifty Caribbean Writers: A Bio-Bibliographical Critical Source book*, Westport, Conn.: Greenwood Press.

— (1990) 'Go Eena Kumbla: A Comparison of Erna Brodber's *Jane and Louisa Will Soon Come Home* and Toni Cade Bambara's *The Salt Eaters*', in Cudjoe (ed.): 169–84.

Dash, Michael (1989) 'In Search of the Lost Body: Re-defining the Subject in Caribbean Literature', *Kunapipi*, 11, 1: 17–26.

Davies, Carole Boyce (1990) '"Woman is a Nation . . ." Women in Caribbean Oral Literature', in Davies and Fido (eds): 165–93.

Davies, Carole Boyce and Elaine Savory Fido (eds) (1990) *Out of the Kumbla: Caribbean Women and Literature*, Trenton, N.J.: Africa World Press.

DeCamp, David (1971) 'Introduction: The Study of Pidgin and Creole Languages', in Dell Hymes (ed.) *Pidginization and Creolization of Languages*, Cambridge: Cambridge University Press: 13–39.

Donnell, Alison (1992) 'Cultural Ambivalence and the Unravelling of Anglo-Centric Narratives in Jamaica Kincaid's Fiction', Paper to Ninth Triennial ACLALS Conference, UWI, Mona, Kingston (August 13–20).

Eagleton, Terry (1983) *Literary Theory: An Introduction*, Oxford: Basil Blackwell.

Esteves, Carmen C. and Lizabeth Paravisini-Gebert (eds) (1991) *Green Cane and Juicy Flotsam: Short Stories by Caribbean Women*, New Brunswick, N.J.: Rutgers.

Evans, Mari (ed.) (1985) *Black Women Writers: Arguments and Interviews*, London and Sydney: Pluto Press.

Farquhar, Bernadette (1981) 'Old and New Creative Writing in Antigua and Barbuda', *Bulletin of Eastern Caribbean Affairs* 7, 5: 29–34.

Feder, Lillian (1980) *Madness in Literature*, Princeton: Princeton University Press.

Fido, Elaine (1990) 'Textures of Third World Reality in the Poetry of Four African-Caribbean Women', in Davies and Fido (eds): 29–44.

— (1991) 'Mother/lands: Self and Separation in the Work of Buchi Emecheta, Bessie Head and Jean Rhys', in Nasta (ed.): 330–49.

Fuss, Diana (1989) *Essentially Speaking: Feminism, Nature and Difference*, London and New York: Routledge.

Garis, Leslie (1990) '"Through West Indian Eyes": Review Article on Jamaica Kincaid', *New York Times Magazine* (October 7): 42–47, 70, 78–80, 91.

Gates, Henry Louis, Jr. (1987) *Figures in Black: Words, Signs and the 'Racial' Self*, Oxford: Oxford University Press.

— (ed.) (1990) *Reading Black, Reading Feminist: A Critical Anthology*, New York: Meridean.

Gikandi, Simon (1989) 'Narration in the Post-Colonial Moment: Merle Hodge's "Crick Crack Monkey"', *Ariel*, 20, 4: 18–30.

Gilbert, Sandra and Susan Gubar (1970) *The Madwoman in the Attic: The Woman Writer and the Nineteenth Century Literary Imagination*, New Haven: Yale University Press.

Gilkes, Michael (1981) *The West Indian Novel*, Boston: Twayne.

Goodison, Lorna (1990) 'How I Became a Writer', in Cudjoe (ed.): 290–3.

Goodwin, Andrew (1988) 'Sample and Hold: Pop Music in the Digital Age of Reproduction', *Critical Quarterly*, 30, 3 (Autumn) 34–49.

Greene, Sue N. (1990) 'Report on the Second International Conference of Caribbean Women Writers', *Callaloo*, 13, 3 (Summer): 532–8.

Griffiths, Gareth (1987) 'Imitation, Abrogation and Appropriation: the production of the post-colonial text', *Kunapipi*, 9, 1: 13–20.

Harris, Claire (1990) 'Mirror, Mirror on the Wall', in Cudjoe (ed.): 306–9.

Harris, Wilson (1967) *Tradition, the Writer and Society: Critical Essays*, London: New Beacon.

Hawthorne, Evelyn (1992) 'Traditions and the Free(d) Subject: A Study of Mary Seacole in post-Emancipation British Culture', Paper to Ninth Triennial ACLALS Conference, UWI, Mona, Kingston (Aug 13–20).

Hebdige, Dick (1987) *Cut 'N' Mix: Culture, Identity and Caribbean Music*, London and New York: Methuen.

Hodge, Merle (1990) 'Challenges of the Struggle for Sovereignty: Changing the World versus Writing Stories', in Cudjoe (ed.): 202–8.

Hutcheon, Linda (1989) '"Circling the Downspout of Empire": Post-Colonialism and Post-Modernism', *Ariel*, 20, 4 (October): 149–75.

Ingersoll, Earl G. (1991) 'Margaret Atwood's "Cat's Eye": Reviewing Women in a Post-Modern World', *Ariel*, 22, 4 (October): 17–27.

JanMohammed, Abdul (1983) *Manichean Aesthetics: The Politics of Literature in Colonial Africa*, Amherst: University of Massachusetts Press.

Johnson, Joyce Walker (1989) 'Autobiography, History, and the Novel: Erna Brodber's *Jane and Louisa Will Soon Come Home*',' *Journal of West Indian Literature*, 3, 1 (January): 47–59.

Johnson, Lemuel (1990) 'A-beng: (Re) Calling the Body In (To) Question', in Davies and Fido (eds.): 111–42.

Katrak, Ketu H. (1989) 'Decolonizing Culture: Toward a Theory for Post-Colonial Women's Texts', *Modern Fiction Studies*, 35, 1 (Spring): 157–79.

Kincaid, Jamaica (1990) 'Jamaica Kincaid and the Modernist Project: An Interview with Selwyn R. Cudjoe', in Cudjoe (ed.): 215–32. Reprinted from *Callaloo*, 12 (Spring 1989): 396–411.

King, Bruce (ed.) (1979) *West Indian Literature*, London: MacMillan.

King-Aribasala, Karen (1992) '"Columbus in Chains": The Voyage as a Cultural Crossing[:] An Analysis of Jamaica Kincaid's *Lucy*', Paper to Ninth Triennial ACLALS Conference, UWI, Mona, Kingston (August 13–20).

Kristeva, Julia (1980) *Desire in Language*, New York: Columbia University Press.

Laing, R.D. (1960) *The Divided Self: A Study of Sanity and Madness*, London: Tavistock.

Lalla, Barbara (1992) 'Womb of Darkness: Journey and Identity in *Wide Sargasso Sea*', Paper to Ninth Triennial ACLALS Conference. UWI, Mona, Kingston (August 13–20).

Ledent, Bénédicte (1992) 'Voyages into Otherness: Recent Fiction by Jamaica Kincaid and Caryl Phillips', Paper to Ninth Triennial ACLALS Conference. UWI, Mona, Kingston (August 13–20).

Look Lai, Wally (1968) 'The Road to Thornfield Hall', *New World Quarterly*, 4, 2: 17–27.

Magnum, Bryant (1986) 'Jamaica Kincaid', in Dance (ed.): 255–63.

Marshall, Paule (1983) 'The Making of a Writer: From the Poets in the Kitchen', Introduction to *Merle and Other Stories*, London: Virago: 3–12.

Mohanty, Chandra (1988) 'Under Western Eyes: Feminist Scholarship and Colonial Discourses', *Feminist Review*, 30: 61–88.

Moi, Toril (1986) 'Feminist Literary Criticism', in *Modern Literary Theory: A Comparative Introduction*, (eds) Ann Jefferson and David Robey, London: B.T. Batsford. Second Edition. 204–221.

— (1991) *Sexual/Textual Politics: Feminist Literary Theory*, London and New York: Routledge. First published 1985.

Mordecai, Pamela (1986) '"A Crystal of Ambiguities": Metaphors for Creativity and the Art of Writing in Derek Walcott's *Another Life*', in *West Indian Poetry: Proceedings of the Fifth Annual Conference on West Indian Literature*, St Thomas: College of the Virgin Islands: 106–21.

Mordecai, Pamela and Betty Wilson (eds) (1989) *Her True – True Name: An Anthology of Women's Writing from the Caribbean*, London: Heinemann.

Morris, Mervyn (1992) 'Cross-Cultural Impersonations: Pauline Melville's *Shape-Shifter*', Paper to Eleventh Annual Conference on West Indian Literature, University of Guyana, Turkeyen Campus (May 31–June 3).

Morrison, Anthea (1990) 'Exile and Homecoming: Maryse Condé's *La Vie Scélérate*', Paper to Second International Conference of Caribbean Women Writers, UWI, St Augustine (April 24–27).

Morrison, Toni (1985) 'Rootedness: The Ancestor as Foundation', in Evans (ed.): 339–45.

Mukherjee, Arun P. (1991) 'The Exclusions of Post-colonial Theory and Mulk Raj Anand's *Untouchable*: A Case Study', *Ariel*, 22, 3 (July): 27–48.

Murdoch, H. Adlai (1992) '(Re)Figuring Colonialism: Narratalogical and Ideological Resistance', *Callaloo*, 15, 1: 2–11.

Nasta, Susheila (ed.) (1991) *Motherlands: Black Women's Writing from Africa, the Caribbean and South Asia*, London: The Women's Press; Brunswick, N.J.: Rutgers, 1992.

Nichols, Grace (1990) 'The Battle with Language', in Cudjoe (ed.): 283–9.

Nunez-Harrell, Elizabeth (1985) 'The Paradoxes of Belonging: The White West Indian Woman in Fiction', *Modern Fiction Studies*, 31, 2 (Summer): 281–93.

O'Callaghan, Evelyn (1985) 'The Bottomless Abyss: "Mad" Women in Some Caribbean Novels', *Bulletin of Eastern Caribbean Affairs,* 11, 1: (March–April): 45–58.

— (1988) 'Feminist Consciousness: European/American Theory, Jamaican Stories', *Journal of Caribbean Studies*, 6, 2 (Spring): 143–62.

— (1990) '"Spirit thievery comes in so many forms": a review of *Myal* by Erna Brodber', *Journal of West Indian Literature*, 4, 1: 50–9.

Paravisini-Gebert, Lizabeth (1992) 'Feminism, Race and Difference in the Works of Mayotte Capécia, Michèle Lacrosil, and Jacqueline Manicom', *Callaloo*, 15, 1: 66–74.

Paravisini, Lizabeth and Barbara Webb (1988) 'On the Threshold of Becoming Caribbean Women Writers', *Cimarrón*, 1, 3: 106–31.

Perry, Donna (1990) 'Initiation in Jamaica Kincaid's *Annie John*', in Cudjoe (ed.): 245–53.

Peterson, Kirsten Holst and Anna Rutherford (eds) (1986) *A Double Colonization: Colonial and Post-Colonial Women's Writing*, Mundelstrup: Dangaroo Press, Foreward: 9–10.

Phaf, Ineke (1990) 'Women Writers of the Dutch-Speaking Caribbean: *Life Long Poem* in the Tradition of Surinamese *Granmorgu*, (New Dawn)', in Cudjoe (ed.): 357–64.

Philip, Marlene Nourbese (1990) 'Managing the Unmanageable', in Cudjoe (ed.): 295–300.

— (1990) 'The Absence of Writing or How I almost Became a Spy', in Davies and Fido (eds): 271–8.

Pollard, Velma (1991) 'Mothertongue Voices in the Writing of Olive Senior and Lorna Goodison', in Nasta (ed.): 238–53.

Poynting, Jeremy (1990) '"You Want to be a Coolie Woman?": Gender and Ethnic Identity in Indo-Caribbean Women's Writing', in Cudjoe (ed.): 98–105.

Pyne Timothy, Helen (1990) 'Adolescent Rebellion and Gender Relations in *At the Bottom of the River* and *Annie John*', in Cudjoe (ed.): 233–42.

Rack, Philip (1982) *Race, Culture and Mental Disorder*. London: Tavistock.

Ramchand, Kenneth (1972) *The West Indian Novel and its Background*, London: Faber.

— (1988) 'West Indian Literary History: Literariness, Orality and Periodization', *Callaloo*, 11, 1: 95–110.

Reddock, Rhoda (1990) 'Feminism, Nationalism, and the Early Women's Movement in the English-Speaking Caribbean (with Special Reference to Jamaica and Trinidad and Tobago)', in Cudjoe (ed.): 61–81.

Rhys, Jean (1979) *Smile Please: An Unfinished Autobiography*, London: André Deutsch.

— (1985) *Letters 1931–66* (eds) Francis Wyndham and Diana Melly, Harmondsworth: Penguin.

Rooney, Caroline (1991) '"Dangerous Knowledge" and the Poetics of Survival: A Reading of *Our Sister Killjoy* and *A Question of Power*', in Nasta (ed.): 99–126.

Senior, Olive (1988) Interview with Charles Rowell, *Callaloo*, 11, 3 (Summer): 480–90.

Shelton, Marie-Denise (1990) 'Women Writers of the French-Speaking Caribbean: An Overview', in Cudjoe ed.: 346–56.

Showalter, Elaine (1977) *A Literature of Their Own: British Women Novelists from Brönte to Lessing*, Princeton, N.J.: Princeton University Press.

Slemon, Stephen (1989) 'Modernism's Last Post', *Ariel*, 20, 4: 3–17.

— (1992) 'Re-turning the Language of Empire', Paper to Ninth Triennial ACLALS Conference, UWI, Mona, Kingston (August 13–20).

Slemon, Stephen and Helen Tiffin (1989) 'Introduction', *Kunapipi*, 11, 1 (Special Issue on Post-Colonial Criticism): ix–xxiii.

Smilowitz, Erica and Roberta Knowles (eds) (1981) *Proceedings of the First Annual Conference on West Indian Literature*, St Thomas: College of the Virgin Islands.

Spivak, Gayatri Chakravorty (1985) 'Three Women's Texts and a Critique of Imperialism', *Critical Inquiry*, 12, 1 (Autumn) 243–61.

Suárez, Isabel Carrera (1991) 'Absent Mother(Land)s: Joan Riley's Fiction', in Nasta (ed.): 290–309.

Tate, Claudia (ed.) (1983) *Black Women Writers at Work*, New York: Continuum.

Thorpe, Marjorie (1977) 'The Problem of Cultural Identification in *Crick Crack Monkey*', *Savacou*, 13: 31–8.

— (1986) 'Challenging the Stereotype: a re-reading of Merle Hodge's *Crick Crack Monkey*', Paper to Sixth Annual Conference on West Indian Literature. University of the West Indies, St Augustine, Trinidad (May).

Tiffin, Helen (1978) 'Mirror and Mask: Colonial Motifs in the Novels of Jean Rhys', *World Literature Written in English*, 17 (April): 328–41.

— (1988) 'Post-Colonialism, Post-Modernism and the Rehabilitation of Post-Colonial History', *Journal of Commonwealth Literature*, 23, 1: 169–81.

— (1989a) 'Rites of Resistance: Counter-Discourse and West Indian Biography', *Journal of West Indian Literature*, 3, 1: 28–46.

— (1989b) Paper to Queen's University, Canada. A revised version appears as 'Decolonization and Audience: Erna Brodber's *Myal* and Jamaica Kincaid's *A Small Place*', in William McGane (ed.) *A Sense of Audience: Essays in Post-Colonial Literature*, Wollangong: SPACLALS (1990): 27–38.

— (1992) 'Travelling Texts: Intertextuality and Resistance', Paper to Ninth Triennial ACLALS Conference, UWI, Mona, Kingston (August 13–20).

Trotter, David (1990) 'Colonial Subjects', *Critical Quarterly*, 32, 3: 3–20.

Walcott, Derek (1989)'Caligula's Horse', *Kunapipi*, 11, 1: 138–42.

Waugh, Patricia (1989) *Feminine Fictions: Revisiting the Post-Modern*, London and New York: Routledge.

Weedon, Chris (1987) *Feminist Practice and Post-Structuralist Theory*, London: Basil Blackwell.

Wilkins, Nadine (1989) 'The Medical Profession in Jamaica in the Post-Emancipation Period', *Jamaica Journal*, 21, 4: 27–32.

Wilson, Betty (1990) 'Claiming an identity they taught me to despise: from Mayotte Capécia to Michele Cliff', Paper to Second International Conference of Caribbean Women Writers, UWI, St Augustine (April 24–27).

— (1991) 'Literature and Life: Female Role Models' and the Socialization of Women in Caribbean Literature', Paper to the Canadian Association of Latin American and Caribbean Studies, Quebec (November).

Wynter, Sylvia (1990a) 'Beyond Miranda's Meanings: Un/silencing the "Demonic Ground" of Caliban's "Woman"', in Davies and Fido (eds): 355–72

— (1990b) 'Towards the Unity of a Caribbean Vision: Reinterpreting 1492–1992', Address to Second International Conference of Caribbean Women Writers, UWI, St Augustine (April 24–27).

Index